heroes

D1501403

JIM STYNES   PAUL CURRIE   JON CARNEGIE

A SUE HINES BOOK
ALLEN & UNWIN

First published in Australia in 2003

Allen & Unwin
83 Alexander Street
Crows Nest NSW 2065
Australia
Phone: (61 2) 8425 0100
Fax: (61 2) 9906 2218
Email: info@allenandunwin.com
Web: www.allenandunwin.com

National Library of Australia
Cataloguing-in-Publication entry:
Stynes, Jim.
    Heroes.

    New ed.
    Bibliography.
    ISBN 1 86508 725 4.

    1. Motivation (Psychology). 2. Youth - Conduct of life.
    3. Youth - Psychology. 4. Achievement motivation in youth.
    I. Carnegie, Jon. II. Currie, Paul. III. Title.

    153.8

Cover, text design and typesetting by MAU Design
Front cover photographs by Lisa Saad
Back cover photographs by Lisa Saad and Austral

Printed in Singapore by Imago Productions
10 9 8 7 6 5 4 3 2

CONTENTS

HEROES ARE JUST ORDINARY PEOPLE ON EXTRAORDINARY JOURNEYS. SURE, SOME PEOPLE ARE BORN WITH GREATER TALENT THAN OTHERS BUT IN THE END IT IS RARELY THE TALENT ALONE THAT BRINGS YOU THROUGH.

IT'S MORE THE ABILITY TO BE INSPIRED BY A DREAM TO GET OUT THERE AND HAVE A GO: TO FOLLOW YOUR HEART AND KEEP MOVING FORWARD EVEN WHEN YOU DOUBT YOURSELF.

CHAPTER 1
THE ORDINARY WORLD

O me! O life!…
of the questions of these recurring;
Of the endless trains of the faithless
—of cities filled with the foolish…
The question, O me! so sad, recurring
—What good amid these, O me, O life?

Answer
That you are here—that life exists, and identity;
That the powerful play goes on,
and you will contribute a verse.

WALT WHITMAN

WHAT STOPS US LEAVING THE ORDINARY WORLD?

THE ORDINARY WORLD IS THE ENVIRONMENT IN WHICH MOST PEOPLE LIVE. IT IS THE PLACE WHERE PEOPLE OFTEN FEEL MOST COMFORTABLE, BUT IS ALSO A PLACE WHERE THEY FEEL THEIR DREAMS CAN BE DRAINED OUT OF THEM. WHILE THE ORDINARY WORLD MAY BE A GREAT PLACE TO REST, IT IS A STIFLING PLACE TO LIVE YOUR DREAMS. IN THE ORDINARY WORLD PEER GROUPS, MEDIA AND FAMILY OFTEN TRY TO HOLD YOU BACK AND PEOPLE CAN GET SO CAUGHT UP IN THE THICK OF THINGS THAT THEY FEEL OVERWHELMED AND SENSE THERE IS NO WAY OUT. WHEN YOU FEEL LIKE THIS IT'S TIME TO TAKE THE FIRST STEP ON THE HERO'S JOURNEY.

PEER PRESSURE

For many teenagers, peer pressure is the single biggest force in their lives. Wanting to belong to a group is such a strong motivation that sometimes young people squash who they really are inside, just to fit in. When you are forced to play a role that doesn't suit you, the results are often devastating. Good peer groups let you be who you are. They let you explore the world and they encourage you to be different. Bad peer groups force you to be someone you are not. You feel like you are acting all the time and are never allowed to be yourself.

MEDIA PRESSURE

Ella Hooper from Killing Heidi knows more about media pressure than most teenagers. She has seen it from both sides. 'The media plays funny games,' she says. 'On one hand they pretend to encourage you to be different and on the other, they want everyone to look and act the same.' Media pressure works very closely with peer pressure in keeping you in your ordinary world. By creating norms which are unobtainable for most people, the media are saying this is what young people should aspire to. The further out of reach the norm is, the harder it is for you to leave your ordinary world. If we all aspired to the life the media portray as real we would never leave the coffee shop.

FAMILY PRESSURE

The family can be both a positive and negative force for motivating you to leave your ordinary world. For most people, their family is their ordinary world and some people's families are so wonderful that they never want to leave. To discover who you are and to gain the courage to go on the hero's journey, you need to be aware of how influential your family is in your life. Very often, the more you love your family the greater the force it places on you. This, in turn, can hold you back.

'THE MEDIA PLAYS FUNNY GAMES. ON ONE HAND THEY PRETEND TO ENCOURAGE YOU TO BE DIFFERENT AND ON THE OTHER, THEY WANT EVERY-ONE TO LOOK AND ACT THE SAME.'
ELLA HOOPER KILLING HEIDI

FOR THE FIRST FEW YEARS OF OUR LIVES,
WE ARE LIKE SPONGES, ABSORBING ALL
THE GOOD AND BAD EXPERIENCES INTO OUR
SUBCONSCIOUS, WITHOUT FILTERING THEM
AS THEY HAPPEN.

BELIEFS=BEHAVIOURS=RESULTS

The longer you stay in the ordinary world, the stronger your beliefs will convince you that you cannot leave it. You will begin to develop lifelong patterns of mediocrity which can lead to a very comfortable life for some, but in the end those who are blessed with a sense of adventure will feel they have missed out if they stay too long in the ordinary world. For the first few years of our lives, we are like sponges, absorbing all the good and bad experiences into our subconscious, without filtering them as they happen. As a result, some of us have very negative beliefs about ourselves, which have originated in childhood.

These limiting beliefs include things like:
I am lazy.
I am disorganised.
I am too shy.
I'll never be good enough to make that team.
I always fail under pressure.
Everyone else gets the breaks except me.

They can even be physical things like:
I'm too tall.
I'm too short.
I'm too weak.
I'm too overweight.
I'm too slow.
I'm not attractive.

When you mix these with peer pressure, family pressure and media pressure, all of which are often telling you the same things, these beliefs can manifest into 'realities'.

All these limiting beliefs, plus the thousands of others we process every day, restrict your capacity to leave your ordinary world. They form subconscious patterns in your brain which lead you to a negative view of the world. For many, this negative view becomes a self-fulfilling prophesy and they feel powerless to change the 'bad luck' that life seems to deal them. Sadly people who harbour these types of negative thoughts tend to hang around together and build a safety network with other negative thinkers. This network is designed to keep you in your ordinary world. It is designed to stop you trying to achieve things, because if you are successful, those around you who never had the courage to try are faced with the awful truth that perhaps life is what you make it rather than what it makes of you!

HERO
ROGER BANNISTER

PERHAPS THE STORY OF MIDDLE DISTANCE RUNNER ROGER BANNISTER BEST ILLUSTRATES HOW BELIEFS CAN AFFECT RESULTS AND KEEP YOU IN THE ORDINARY WORLD.

For thousands of years, no athlete had ever broken the four minute mile barrier for running. It was deemed impossible until the British runner Roger Bannister did it in 1954. While this was an enormous personal achievement for Bannister it was also a great achievement for athletics.

After thousands of years of believing it was impossible to break the four minute mile, suddenly Bannister had done it. That same year a further 37 runners also broke the four minute mile and the following year another 300 beat it as well.

believe

BELIEFS BEHAVIOURS RESULTS

To escape the ordinary world you have to start questioning where your limiting beliefs come from. For most of us the answers will lie in our families, peers and the media. Have a look at the examples below and then make a list of your own.

LIMITING BELIEF
I'm not good enough.
WHERE DID IT COME FROM?
A father who continually told you that you were no good?

LIMITING BELIEF
I hate myself.
WHERE DID IT COME FROM?
Always trying to win your parents' approval and never getting it?

LIMITING BELIEF
I'm a failure.
WHERE DID IT COME FROM?
Always being compared to your older brother or sister?

For most of us these limiting beliefs will form patterns in our minds because of the questions we ask ourselves each day. These questions are subconsciously structured to bring us the same answers all the time. For example the question, 'Why am I a failure?' assumes that you are a failure! Try rephrasing the question and ask, 'What can I do to become a success?' Suddenly you are empowered. This question assumes you have control over you destiny!

The capacity to change the questions you ask yourself is the key to turning limiting beliefs into empowering ones. And you can do that right now.

LIMITING BELIEFS

On a piece of paper write down what your life's dream is right now.

EXAMPLE
– I want to be an Oscar-winning actor.

Now write down all the limiting beliefs you have about being an Oscar-winning actor.

EXAMPLES
– It's too hard to get a part in a Hollywood movie.
– I am not attractive enough to be an actor.
– Only blockbuster movies win Academy Awards and I want to do musicals.

Now write down a set of questions which help make your dream become clear and achievable to you.

– What can I do to become an Oscar-winning actor?
– What steps do I have to take to get a part in a Hollywood movie?
– How can I be in musicals and still win an Academy Award?

Just by asking these questions you are starting to think positively about your dream.

Of course just asking the questions is not enough. You have to act on them as well. And this is where the hero's journey becomes very real. There is no such thing as instant success in the hero's journey. For many who start on the journey of becoming an Oscar-winning actor, the process will help them redefine the goal as they go along. Instead of becoming an actor, they find out their passion lies in directing or writing and their journey changes. The key to success here is to keep doing things that make you happy, but to understand that happiness is not easy to find. Sometimes you have to go through hundreds of failures before you discover the thing that truly makes you happy. Thomas Edison, for example, discovered dozens of ways not to make a light bulb before he actually developed one which worked!

START NOW!

TO ACHIEVE SUCCESS ON THE HERO'S JOURNEY, START NOW.

RIGHT THIS SECOND.

ASK NEW QUESTIONS TO CHANGE THE LIMITING BELIEFS YOU HAVE.

LIMITING BELIEF:
IT IS IMPOSSIBLE FOR ME TO BECOME AN OSCAR-WINNING ACTOR?

NEW QUESTION:
WHAT CAN I DO TO BECOME AN OSCAR-WINNING ACTOR?

NEW BELIEF:
IT IS REALLY HARD WORK TO BECOME AN OSCAR-WINNING ACTOR, BUT THERE IS NOTHING STOPPING ME STARTING THE JOURNEY, SO WHY NOT JUST START?

DIG A LITTLE DEEPER
- A STEP ALONG THE WAY

DAVID'S STORY

For many people, removing limiting beliefs takes a lot of practice and sometimes it takes years to master. The reason for this is that often the behaviour that causes these limiting beliefs has served us well in our lives. For example, David's behaviour is common in young people who suffered abuse as children.

'When I was young, my dad used to get drunk and beat up both me and my mum. I hated him for doing it, but as I grew older I began to use violence myself to solve problems. It actually felt good to get into fights and even better when I won them. So my regular Saturday night always involved drinking and fighting. It wasn't until I was summonsed to appear in court and I was standing in the docks explaining to the judge why I couldn't stop fighting that I realised I sounded exactly like my father; exactly like the man I hated. That's when I knew I had to change. When you get to that point in your life, it often gives you enough strength to follow through with the change. Even now I still get angry really easy, but now when it happens I ask myself a new question: "Do I want to end up like my father?" I know the answer to that is no. So what I thought was an uncontrollable urge to fight has now become a controllable urge not to become my own person; to discover who I am and not to play the victim all the time.'

If we are not getting the results in life we want in our ordinary world, it suggests we have a limiting belief of some kind and in order to remove this we first need to become aware of it so then we can gain a clearer understanding of the belief and where it came from. When we acknowledge its negative influence we can then put it to rest and develop a more positive belief about the situation.

Remember, a lot of what we believe has been learned from our parents, which is not necessarily a good thing! A lot of people never really question why they act the way they do, they just know that other people act the same way and that's why they do it. It might well be, however, that they simply don't know there are other ways of behaving.

The hero's journey is all about expanding your beliefs so that you have a better map to help you navigate life's evolving roadways. If you were travelling to a difficult destination, then you would definitely want a good map to guide you.

TO CHANGE A LIMITING BELIEF, YOU NEED TO UNDERSTAND WHERE IT CAME FROM.

The only person who can change your limiting beliefs is you.

In order to change your limiting beliefs you must be prepared to be proactive in accepting responsibility for the task. Changing beliefs is easy, but maintaining the change is very hard. Sometimes we have developed beliefs which protected us as young people, but now, as we are getting older, they no longer serve us as Carley's story tells us.

'When I was eight my father walked out on us. I was so hurt I decided never to allow myself to trust another man again. When my mum got a new boyfriend, even though he was really nice, I did not feel like I could trust him and I never let him get close to me. This really hurt him and my mum. Even now after six years, I still have not accepted him.

'I guess my hero's journey is to overcome the limiting belief that men can't be trusted. When I was a kid, the belief protected me, but now, even though I still can't do it, I can see how destructive my belief is on my family and I know I have to change it. By letting my father's actions affect me eight years after they happened, I am still letting him have control over me.'

In other words, if you want to move forward on the hero's journey you have to start responding to who you are and not reacting to who others 'force' you to be.

IN ORDER TO CHANGE YOUR LIMITING BELIEFS YOU MUST BE PREPARED TO BE PROACTIVE IN ACCEPTING RESPONSIBILITY FOR THE TASK. CHANGING BELIEFS IS EASY, BUT MAINTAINING THE CHANGE IS VERY HARD.

THE QUESTION 'WHO ARE YOU?' IS ONE THAT CAN BE ANSWERED ON MANY DIFFERENT LEVELS. FOR SOME PEOPLE, THE ANSWER IS AS SIMPLE AS GIVING THEIR NAME, WHILE FOR OTHERS THE ANSWER IS A LOT MORE COMPLEX. TO REALLY DISCOVER WHO YOU ARE, YOU NEED TO BE AWARE OF THE WHOLE RANGE OF FORCES WHICH HAVE SHAPED YOU. AS WE HAVE DISCUSSED, PEERS, FAMILY AND MEDIA ARE BIG INFLUENCES IN DETERMINING WHO YOU ARE, BUT FOR THE MOST PART THEY ARE ALL ASSOCIATED WITH THE EGO VERSION OF WHO YOU ARE.

THE REAL YOU IS NOT REFLECTED IN WHAT OTHER PEOPLE THINK YOU ARE. THE REAL YOU IS LOCKED IN YOUR SPIRIT. AS YOU GET OLDER, IT BECOMES INCREASINGLY DIFFICULT TO UNLOCK YOUR SPIRIT BECAUSE YOU HAVE SPENT SO LONG TRYING TO FIT IN WITH OTHERS.

REMEMBER BACK TO WHEN YOU WERE VERY YOUNG. IF SOMEONE ASKED YOU WHAT YOU WANTED TO BE, YOUR IMAGINATION WENT WILD. YOUNG KIDS WANT TO BE ASTRONAUTS, PILOTS, SAILORS AND ROCK STARS, AND IT IS ONLY AS THEY GET OLDER THAT THESE DREAMS ARE SLOWLY TAKEN AWAY FROM THEM. IT IS ONLY WHEN WE START LISTENING TO OUR EGO AND NOT OUR SPIRIT THAT THINGS SEEM TO GO OFF TRACK.

WHO ARE YOU?

Knowing who you are helps to give you the strength to make good decisions when faced by pressures from your peer group or the media.

TAKE THE STORY OF A GROUP OF 17-YEAR-OLD SCHOOL FRIENDS WHO DECIDED TO TAKE A JOY RIDE. THESE BOYS HAD THE WORLD AT THEIR FEET. YOUNG, ATHLETIC AND SMART, THEY WERE DESTINED FOR GREAT LIVES. THEY MADE THE SAME DECISION MANY YOUNG PEOPLE MAKE. THEY GOT INTO AN OVERCROWDED CAR WITH AN UNLICENSED DRIVER. MINUTES LATER, WHEN THE CAR VEERED OFF THE ROAD AND HIT A PAPERBARK TREE, THREE OF THEM WERE DEAD.

Was it worth the risk? Only you can answer that question.
Would you have got into the car? Again, only you can answer that question.
What will you do when you are faced with the same situation?

Understanding who you are will help you answer questions on risk-taking. If your answer to any of the above questions is yes, take into account the following stories of parents whose children died that day. The driver was sentenced to two years. Meanwhile, three families face life sentences, with no remissions for good behaviour. They do their time hard.

Every week, the father of one of the boys goes to the cemetery to talk to his son. The other two families live through the pain on a daily basis.

All young people make mistakes, but thinking about the consequences of their actions can give them the strength to limit their risk-taking.

Some years on, the tree the boys hit has been cut down. Only a sandy mound marks the spot where a stupid kid in a car smashed so many lives. Soon the grass will heal the scarred ground. Broken hearts do not mend so easily.

Knowledge of who you are allows you to make decisions without being overly influenced by peers and media. It gives you a balanced approach to risk-taking and it puts you in control.

UNDERSTANDING THE DIFFERENCE BETWEEN EGO AND SPIRIT

The need for acceptance versus the need to be me is the internal war, ego versus spirit. To begin the hero's journey we need to understand these parts of ourselves: our ego and our spirit.

A simple way to describe the ego is as that little voice inside your head that dictates the way you act and the way you want to be seen in public. It is your ego more than anything that keeps you within your comfort zone and stops you from breaking out and being yourself around others.

Watch anyone driving alone in a car singing at the top of their lungs with the radio turned full on full blast. As long as they can't see you, they are dreaming of being a rock star or the hero of the song breaking free, but as soon as they see you watching, what do they do?

They stop!

The voice inside their head causes them to get embarrassed. They pretend to wipe their mouths as though they were just yawning and they look the other way. They stop dreaming, they feel uncomfortable and they withdraw back to their comfort zone while their spirit is left high and dry with nothing to sing about any more.

People with spirit, however, are not afraid to sing out loud or dance the way they feel. In the documentary, *Lionheart*, directed by Paul Currie, Jesse Martin spent hours on his boat playing guitar and singing to himself.

'It was exhilarating' says Jesse, 'singing with no one there to judge you, or to tell you that you sound awful. I know I can't sing well, but I can sing and I love doing it. The real challenge came when Paul told me he wanted to use the singing in the documentary. I knew thousands of people would be watching it and I knew it sounded terrible. It took me some time to come to terms with the fact that it was only my ego which was stopping me from letting Paul use the tape. Looking back I'm really glad we did. I was singing from the heart and you should never be embarrassed about that.'

IT IS YOUR EGO MORE THAN ANYTHING THAT KEEPS YOU WITHIN YOUR COMFORT ZONE AND STOPS YOU FROM BREAKING OUT AND BEING YOURSELF AROUND OTHERS.

'IT WAS AN ADVENTURE I HAD DREAMT OF ALL MY LIFE AND IF WE DON'T LIVE OUR DREAMS, WHAT'S THE POINT OF LIVING?'

HERO

JESSE MARTIN

WHEN 17-YEAR-OLD JESSE MARTIN LEFT HIS ORDINARY WORLD, HE WENT ON AN ADVENTURE THAT CHANGED HIS LIFE AND THE LIVES OF THOUSANDS OF OTHERS. ACCORDING TO JESSE MARTIN THE THING THAT ENCOURAGED HIM TO LEAVE HIS ORDINARY WORLD MORE THAN ANYTHING ELSE WAS HIS DISSATISFACTION WITH THE WAY HIS LIFE WAS GOING AT THE TIME.

'Although I was enjoying school, it wasn't really offering me the opportunities I was seeking. And although I don't really understand why I chose to do it, leaving school to go off and sail around the world was a choice. It was an adventure I had dreamt of all my life and if we don't live our dreams, what's the point of living? So on 7 December 1998, I set out to become the youngest person ever to circumnavigate the globe, solo, nonstop and unassisted.

Funnily enough in the lead-up to the whole thing, I never really had any fear. It wasn't until I was actually on the boat and sailing that I began to think to myself, "Jesus, I am really doing this, I can't turn back now." Up until then there had always been safety nets, but once I was out on the water and sailing that was it. I can distinctly remember cutting the motor as I sailed out of Port Phillip Bay and heard for the first time the sounds of my new home for the next eleven months. There were no real fanfares or anything like that, just my dad in the distance on his small catamaran, a distant group of observers and the ocean in front of me.

Looking back now, what's funny is, once I was on the water, I didn't really give a shit about the record. The record was just a way of raising money, the real reason was I just wanted to do it. There were heaps of people telling me how dangerous it was and stuff, but the people who really mattered, like my parents, supported me and that was all I needed.

In the first few days, the main fear I experienced was fear of the unknown. Fear of failure, fear of the unexpected, and probably that was the hardest time, but it was also the time of most hope. Even when the boat got tipped in really big weather, although I was scared, I could cope with that fear better, because it was out of my control and in a way that's easier to cope with than the actual starting out, when it would have been so easy to make an excuse and not do the journey.

I guess that's where my story is most relevant to the hero's journey. Not that what I achieved was that great, but that I gave it a go. At least I left my ordinary world and tried something different. In many ways the trip was nothing like I imagined it would be.

I remember now, the night before I landed back in Australia, it was not the feeling I had anticipated. I imagined it would be this great relief to finally get home, but, as I said in my book, the journey didn't end, it just kind of fizzled out. And in a way, that was my lesson about the hero's journey. On reaching the end, the myth was really gone. Even though there was this big crowd and everything, and everyone was saying how amazing the trip must have been, inside I didn't really feel very special at all. I don't see myself as a hero, I just did what came naturally to me. That was my journey. The next one may not work, that's OK, we'll just wait and see.'

'SHE LED BY SERVING AND SHOWED US THE STUNNING POWER OF SIMPLE HUMILITY.'

BILL CLINTON FORMER PRESIDENT OF AMERICA, ON MOTHER TERESA.

HOW DO YOU WANT TO BE REMEMBERED?

Imagine for a minute you are walking down the aisle of a church and at the end of that aisle there is a coffin. The pews on either side of you are filled with the familiar faces of your friends and family, but none of them can see you. You approach the coffin, look inside and come face to face with yourself.

Then your best friend gets up and walks to the front of the church near the altar and proceeds to share your life with those present. What would you like this person to say about you?

Start living the life you want to live right now! It will not be easy but the more you do it, the greater the control you will have along the way. Many of you are reading this and thinking 'How could a person like me who has nothing special about them ever achieve the things I want in life? What makes me so different?' The answer is simply the fact that you choose to start. So many people ask exactly those questions and stop right there. They settle for a life of mediocrity and they never even start the hero's journey.

SOMETIMES THE START OF OUR JOURNEY IS TO DISCOVER WE ARE NOT LIVING THE LIFE OF THE PERSON WE WANT TO BE.

What would you say if someone offered you this deal?

Imagine any career you want and if you really want to be that thing and you are prepared to work at it for ten years, your dream is guaranteed to come true. What would you choose to do in life?

Your answer is the starting point on the hero's journey.

You see, if you are realistic about the exercise, there is no reason why the career or life path you have chosen should not suit you. Most likely the only thing stopping you from going for it right now is your ego!

Part of the journey is understanding that your spirit is destined for greater things than your ego will acknowledge.

It's not that it will come easily, but it will come – and the more positive you are about making it happen the more likely it is to happen.

So in the words of the Dead Poets Society, 'Carpe Diem – seize the day – make your lives extraordinary.'

HERE'S HOW...

All of us have a voice inside that believes we are destined for something special in this world. We all harbour the dream that we can make a difference to our own lives and the lives of others, but the older we get the more the dream is washed away by the waves of uncertainty and fear. We develop thought processes which stop us from thinking with our hearts and spirits.

Take a minute now to close your eyes and look into your heart and see if you can reclaim the person you want to be. Perhaps even write down the words as they come into your body. Try to avoid thinking with your head.

Once you have completed this, write out a brief description of the person you would like to be.

Question: Why aren't you that person?

Is it because you're afraid of what other people will think?

Ask yourself if this could this be the greatest challenge in your life. To realise the need to be yourself is more important than the need for acceptance.

It is the capacity to be true to yourself above all other things that will determine your success in life. This quality alone will help you stand out where others fall. The capacity to know who you are helps make the really hard decisions easy in life. That doesn't mean they are easy to follow through, but they are easy to make if you ask yourself these simple questions each time you are faced with a tough decision.

Who am I?

What do I stand for?

What is right in this set of circumstances?

DRIVEN BY A VISION SO STRONG, MANDELA LEFT HIS ORDINARY WORLD AND BEGAN A JOURNEY THAT WAS TO CHANGE THE COURSE OF WORLD HISTORY.

HERO

NELSON MANDELA

WHEN NELSON MANDELA WAS BORN ON 18 JULY 1918, HIS ORDINARY WORLD WAS A TINY VILLAGE ON THE BANKS OF THE MBASHE RIVER IN THE TRANSKEI, EAST OF CAPE TOWN, SOUTH AFRICA.

During his early years, Mandela grew up as a farm boy, herding cattle with the other local boys in his area. He lived in a simple grass hut with his family until the age of nine, when, after the death of his father, he was sent away from his family to live with his uncle who was a wealthy magistrate.

Under the guidance of his uncle, Mandela began to see the great injustices of the society into which he had been born. Driven by a vision so strong, Mandela left his ordinary world and began a journey that was to change the course of world history.

After joining a group called the ANC Mandela set about trying to gain equal rights for the black population of South Africa. For his efforts, Mandela was arrested and placed in jail.

It is at times such as these in our lives that the hero's journey is tested and we begin to discover the real motives behind who we are and why we do things. After being arrested, Mandela could have turned back to his family, he could have listened to the media who called him a terrorist, he could have renounced the ANC and gone back to his friends and their farming communities.

Instead Mandela found his true calling in life and in this extract from his biography, *Long Walk To Freedom*, Mandela explains the conviction required to drive a boy from the ordinary world of farming to become the president of his nation.

'I am prepared to pay the penalty even though I know how bitter and desperate the situation is for an African in prison in this country…Nevertheless, these discriminations do not sway me from the path that I have taken, nor will they sway others like me. For to men, freedom in their own land is the pinnacle of their ambition from which nothing can turn men of conviction aside. More powerful than my fear of the dreadful conditions to which I might be subjected in prison is my hatred for the dreadful conditions to which my people are subjected outside prison throughout this country…

Whatever sentence Your Worship sees fit to impose upon me for the crime for which I have been convicted before this court, may it rest assured that when my sentence has been completed I will still be moved, as men are always moved, by their conscience; I will still be moved by my dislike of the race discrimination against my people when I come out from serving my sentence, to take up again, as best I can, the struggle for removal of those injustices until they are finally abolished once and for all…'

As Nelson Mandela's story shows us, it takes huge courage and personal resilience to be who you are. We need to be resilient to peer, media and family pressure, but that's only the start. There are many other pressures which will impact upon you during your hero's journey. In the following section we will be looking at two movies, *Billy Elliott* and *Dead Poets Society*. Both movies are about individuals trying to discover who they are and to attempt their own hero's journey, while the forces around them try to keep in their ordinary worlds. Try watching both films and using the text to help, see if you can track the hero's journey taken by each of the characters.

'ALWAYS BE
TRUE TO
YOURSELF BILLY.
ALWAYS!'

FILM
BILLY ELLIOTT

BILLY ELLIOTT'S ORDINARY WORLD IS WORKING CLASS NORTHERN ENGLAND DURING THE THATCHER REGIME. BILLY IS BORN INTO A MALE-DOMINATED FAMILY WHERE THE ORDINARY THING FOR BOYS HIS AGE IS TO JOIN THE LOCAL BOXING CLUB. UNFORTUNATELY, BILLY'S ORDINARY WORLD IS NOT ONE HE LIKES AND INSTEAD OF BOXING BILLY BECOMES FASCINATED WITH THE BALLET LESSONS TAKING PLACE NEXT DOOR. IT IS HERE THAT BILLY'S JOURNEY BEGINS. SO WHAT IS IT THAT DRIVES YOUNG BILLY ELLIOTT, THE SON OF A COAL MINER, TO WALK INTO THE BALLET SCHOOL?

At this point in his hero's journey, Billy has to overcome all the pressures placed on him by society and follow his spirit into the ballet school. On entering the room, Billy risks the ridicule of the girls, the wrath of his father and alienation from his friends, but none of this is enough to stop him.

This is the courage it often takes to leave the ordinary world, when the internal voice says, 'This is who I am.'

While Billy's decision to join the ballet class caused many initial conflicts, in the end his actions inspired all those around him. By leaving the ordinary world where so many others felt trapped, Billy Elliott became a symbol of hope and light for others to follow in his extraordinary footsteps.

Watch the movie *Billy Elliott* and see if you can identify the following stages of the hero's journey.

ORDINARY WORLD *Strike-torn mining town.*

CALL TO ADVENTURE *Seeing the ballet school next door to his boxing gym.*

SPECIAL WORLD *Entering the ballet class.*

ENEMIES *His father, brother and friends.*

ALLIES *His ballet teacher, his best friend, his dead mother.*

SLAYING THE DRAGON *Auditioning for the Royal Ballet.*

REWARD *Billy becomes a symbol of hope for his family and community and wins the respect of his father.*

'SEIZE THE DAY.
MAKE YOUR LIVES EXTRAORDINARY.'

FILM
DEAD POETS SOCIETY

NEIL IS AN UPPER-CLASS AMERICAN SCHOOLBOY ATTENDING ONE OF AMERICA'S MOST PRESTIGIOUS PRIVATE SCHOOLS. FOLLOWING IN THE FOOTSTEPS OF HIS FAMOUS BROTHER, NEIL'S ORDINARY WORLD IS SET IN STONE FOR HIM BY HIS DICTATORIAL FATHER, WHO TRIES TO RUN HIS LIFE.

The ordinary world of Welton Academy is the epitome of strict private schools designed to railroad their students into the 'Ivy League' of American colleges.

When Neil meets his English teacher, Mr Keating, himself a former student, he is told to 'seize the day' and make his life extraordinary. The passionate words call out to Neil in a way his father could never do. Mr. Keating awakens Neil's passion to be an actor, but knowing his father would never approve, Neil is faced with two major questions: does he pursue his dream of acting and let his father down, or does he stay in his ordinary would and do as his father demands?

The dilemma is one faced by many who undertake the hero's journey. Not living up to the expectations of friends, family and social standards can often lead to conflict on your journey. During these times it is important to remember that the journey is your journey, not the journey of your parents or peers. While they may be good mentors, they also must set you free to follow your dreams.

Watch the movie *Dead Poets Society* and see if you can follow Neil's journey as set out below.

ORDINARY WORLD Welton Academy.

CALL TO ADVENTURE Seize the day. Neil is inspired by his English teacher.

SPECIAL WORLD Forming Dead Poets Society and deciding to attend play rehearsals.

ENEMIES School culture and his father.

ALLIES His teacher, Mr. Keating, and his friend, Todd.

TESTS Joining the Dead Poets Society. Defying his father. Facing his father. Auditioning for the play.

SUMMARY
THE ORDINARY WORLD

THE ORDINARY WORLD IS THE COMFORT ZONE OF LIFE.

PEER PRESSURE INFLUENCES WHO YOU ARE.

MEDIA PRESSURE INFLUENCES WHO YOU ARE.

FAMILY PRESSURE INFLUENCES WHO YOU ARE.

THE RELATIONSHIP BETWEEN BELIEFS, BEHAVIOURS AND RESULTS DETERMINES YOUR SUCCESS.

THE ESSENTIAL QUESTION IS 'WHO AM I?'

IT TAKES COURAGE TO BE WHO YOU ARE.

YOU NEED PERSONAL RESILIENCE.

CHAPTER 2
THE CALL TO ADVENTURE

Sons of Scotland, I am William Wallace...
and I see a whole army of my countrymen
here in defiance of tyranny.
You've come to fight as free men
and free men you are.
What will you do with that freedom?
Will you fight?
Fight and you may die.
Run and you'll live; at least for a while.
And dying in your beds many years from now,
would you be willing to trade all the days
from that day to now for one chance,
just one chance
to come back here
and tell our enemies
that they may take our lives
but they will never take our freedom!

WILLIAM WALLACE 'BRAVEHEART'

THE FIRST STEP OF ANY JOURNEY IS OFTEN THE HARDEST. SOMETIMES IT TAKES A MAJOR EVENT IN YOUR LIFE TO MOTIVATE YOU INTO ACTION, BUT BEFORE THAT OCCURS, YOU NEED TO ACCEPT RESPONSIBILITY FOR YOUR LOT IN LIFE WHETHER IT IS FAIR OR NOT. THIS IS OFTEN VERY DIFFICULT BECAUSE BAD LUCK AND TRAGEDY CAN STRIKE WITHOUT WARNING. WHEN UNFAIR THINGS HAPPEN TO YOU, IT IS VERY DIFFICULT NOT TO FEEL SORRY FOR YOURSELF, BUT THE REALITY IS UNFAIR THINGS HAPPEN TO EVERYONE. LIFE IS NOT ALWAYS FAIR AND WHEN SOMETHING BAD HAPPENS TO YOU, THE ONLY WAY TO ENDURE IT IS TO CONTROL YOUR RESPONSE.

BY CONTROLLING YOUR RESPONSES AND ALIGNING YOUR ACTIONS WITH A PURPOSE, YOU CAN DEVELOP THE RESILIENCE TO ENDURE THE EARLY PART OF YOUR JOURNEY WHILE ALL THE FORCES DISCUSSED IN CHAPTER 1 ARE IMPACTING AGAINST YOU. SOMETIMES, ACCEPTING RESPONSIBILITY FOR YOUR OWN ACTIONS MAY MEAN GOING TO GET HELP. AT OTHER TIMES IT MEANS SETTING OUT ON YOUR OWN ADVENTURE TO THE SPECIAL WORLD.

HERO
BRYCE COURTENAY

FOR AUTHOR BRYCE COURTENAY, HIS CALL TO ADVENTURE CAME WHEN HE WAS FACED WITH LOSING HIS ONLY SON, WHO HAD CONTRACTED AIDS FROM A BLOOD TRANSFUSION. IN THE FOLLOWING EXTRACT FROM HIS BEST-SELLING BOOK, April Fools' Day, BRYCE EXPLAINS HOW HE HAD NO CHOICE BUT TO ACCEPT THE DEATH OF HIS SON AND THEN BE INSPIRED BY THE LESSONS HE LEARNED ON THE JOURNEY.

'We all thought Damon would die sometime over the Easter long weekend, though, God knows he'd beaten the odds often enough before. The mighty Damon, just when you thought he was a goner, he would make it around the final corner on wobbly legs and totter down the home straight to be back with us again. But each time it was harder and each time he was weaker, a little bit of his old self left behind…

It was Celeste, more than any of us, who had watched his body slowly deteriorate, his ribs growing sharply more pronounced under his taut translucent skin and his limbs becoming so thin and dry that it seemed as though they might snap when he was lifted into bed…

Then on April Fools' Day, a day which began with surprising, unexpected colour, Damon was ready. There was no colour left in him at all, he'd wrung the last drop out, used the last tiny bit to whisper that he loved us.

It was a great effort for us to talk and each of us took our turn in moving up close. "I love you very much, Dad." There was nothing more to say. It was everything contained in one thing, his whole life.

'JUST WHEN YOU THOUGHT HE WAS A GONER, HE WOULD MAKE IT AROUND THE FINAL CORNER ON WOBBLY LEGS AND TOTTER DOWN THE HOME STRAIGHT TO BE BACK WITH US AGAIN.'

'PERHAPS IT REQUIRES SUCH DEPTHS OF OPPRESSION TO CREATE SUCH HEIGHTS OF CHARACTER.'
NELSON MANDELA

LIFE IS A CHALLENGE

One of the great lessons learned on the hero's journey is that life is a challenge. No matter who you are and where you were born, life will inevitably throw challenges your way. For some like Nelson Mandela, those challenges are enormous. For others they are less so. It is the capacity to endure these challenges and learn from them that will often become your greatest attribute.

Through suffering and loss and sadness we learn that we should never take for granted the things we have. Rather, we learn to recognise, respect and use them on our journey. It is perhaps the toughest lesson of all on the hero's journey and one many people question. The faith required to move forward in times of disaster, doubt or despair is one of the great tests people face in their lives.

While the events themselves are not fair, the results of tragic events often lead people to find a strength inside themselves they never knew existed. After the loss of a loved one, for example, it is not unusual for the immediate friends or family of that person to dedicate a period of time – sometimes even their whole lives – to helping others cope with grief. Bryce Courtenay decided to write a book about it so that others could find comfort in his words; Nelson Mandela dedicated his life to the pursuit of freedom for his people. What will your call to adventure inspire you to do?

CHALLENGES ARE BOTH POSITIVE AND NEGATIVE

HERO

DANI DI TORO

TAKE THE STORY OF CHAMPION WHEELCHAIR ATHLETE, DANI DI TORO. DANI'S CALL TO ADVENTURE CAME WHEN SHE WAS JOLTED OUT OF HER ORDINARY WORLD BY A COLLAPSING BRICK WALL.

'For me 15 March 1988 was one of those freaky days where everything was telling me not to go to the Dandenong pool to watch my school swimming sports. Because I can't swim for shit, my best friend and I had decided to wag that day and right up until the last minute, we were fully not going to go – but for some reason we chickened out.

As it turned out, I ended up staying on even after my heats had finished. Even though I was busting to go to the toilet, I decided to stay for one more race to watch my friend swim. It was then, just as the gun went off, that the brick wall under which we were sitting collapsed in – like this total noise – with people screaming all over the place. There was no time to do anything. Before I knew it, the wall was upon me and a large brick block had fallen across my spine.

I can remember looking around, fully conscious and aware of what was going on. I couldn't feel my legs and I can even remember looking up at the ambulance man when he arrived and asking him if he thought it was just spinal shock!

I spent the next four months in hospital trying to come to terms with what had happened to me, and during that time there were many highs and lows. At the start, I was asking myself the usual "what if" questions like, "What if I had gone to the toilet?" and "What if I had wagged that day?" But eventually I had to come to the realisation that nothing was going to change the events of the past and the most important thing now was to concentrate on the future.

From that moment on I decided I would not allow myself to lay blame or wallow in self-pity. Instead I focussed the best I could on getting better and getting back to school.

At times in hospital I did find it hard, especially when I thought of things like the fact that I would never again feel sand between my toes, or climb a tree, or go roller blading or even a simple thing like sitting on a roof. But whenever I started to feel like this, all I had to do was look around and see the quads in my ward who would never even be able to brush their own teeth, or give someone a hug.

I ended up getting out of hospital two months early, and before I knew it I was back in school. From there I went on to do a degree at La Trobe University and then, to become a facilitator for Reach.

Along the way, I also took up wheelchair tennis and I am currently ranked number two in the world. But—as my accident has taught me—you must always be aware that at any moment things can change. I may, or I may not become number one in the world, but to me it's not the ranking that is so important, as the fact that whatever I do, I am doing it to the best of my ability.

So, although many people might like to think my call to adventure has led me to become a world-ranked tennis player, I would like to think it has done much more than that. For me, tennis is just a part of a greater journey which is to be the best me I can be. To be true to my potential; to respect who I am and what I can give, so that when I finally leave this earth they won't just say "There goes Dani Di Toro, number one wheelchair tennis player in the world." They'll say "There goes Dani Di Toro, who was not afraid to be true to who she really was."'

Clearly what happened to Dani was a negative event, but with a positive attitude she has managed to turn things around. If anything, challenges in our life are often the wake-up calls we need to appreciate what we have been taking for granted.

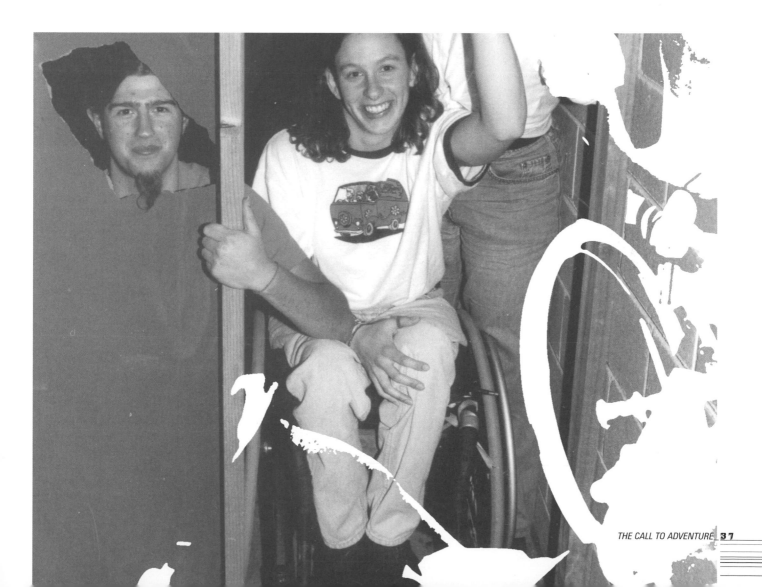

DONT TAKE LIFE FOR GRANTED

Learning not to take things for granted is a big part of the hero's journey. Too many of us confuse the things we want with the things we need. For example, if we were to list all the things we could ever want to get us through life and help us achieve our dreams, most of us would be getting into the hundreds before we started to list things that we didn't already have. If you don't believe this, try living your dreams without some of the following and you will get the idea: air, water, sight, hearing, touch, smell, taste, food, shelter, friendship, love, happiness, health, sanity, a smile...

So often your call to adventure comes only when you lose one of these things, making you realise how important and valuable these things are. We cannot really go after our dreams until we begin to appreciate all of the good things we have in life. A lot of us often forget that no matter how bad things become for us, we all have a lifetime of great opportunities ahead of us.

Try making a mental list of all the good things you already have in life. When you have done this why not write them down and stick them on a mirror at home to remind you on a daily basis how good life really is.

INDIVIDUAL RESPONSIBILITY

This is a true story. David, Leanne and Janet are at a party. After four hours drinking together they decide to leave. As they near Leanne's car, David asks her if she is OK to drive. She replies that she feels fine and she hasn't had a drink for ages.

Looking across at the taxi queue which is a mile long, David accepts her story and climbs into the back of the car, while Janet gets in the front with Leanne. Minutes later, Leanne turns into a busy main road and proceeds to drive when suddenly she notices a set of headlights approaching from the opposite direction.

The accident resulted in the death of her friend and the other driver. Leanne had pulled into oncoming traffic. Her blood alcohol was three times the legal limit. It was her third drink-driving offence and even after the accident and the death of her friend, Leanne still maintains she had been 'OK to drive'. David, who survived in the back seat, claimed he had believed Leanne when she had said she was OK to drive.

Taking individual responsibility for your actions takes enormous honesty. You have to be prepared to accept the consequences of your actions and not allow others to draw you into behaviour you know is wrong.

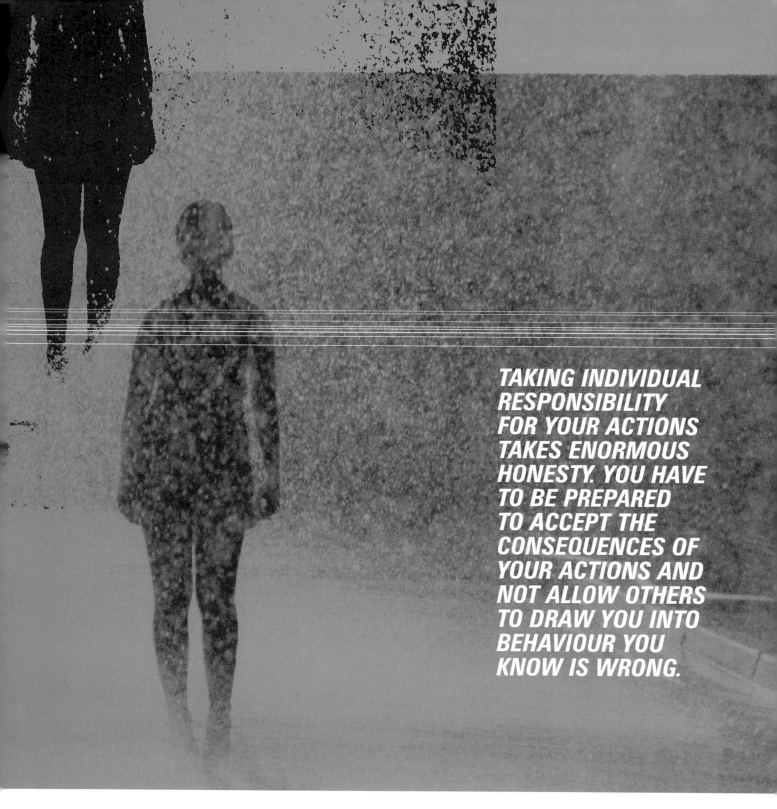

TAKING INDIVIDUAL RESPONSIBILITY FOR YOUR ACTIONS TAKES ENORMOUS HONESTY. YOU HAVE TO BE PREPARED TO ACCEPT THE CONSEQUENCES OF YOUR ACTIONS AND NOT ALLOW OTHERS TO DRAW YOU INTO BEHAVIOUR YOU KNOW IS WRONG.

INSPIRE

'I ALWAYS WANTED TO MOTIVATE AND INSPIRE, TO MAKE A DIFFERENCE IN THIS WORLD. BUT I NEVER KNEW HOW. NOW I FEEL AS THOUGH I'M ON THIS EARTH FOR A REASON AND THAT I'M GOING TO DO MY DARNEDEST TO HELP THE YOUTH OF THIS COUNTRY.'

HERO

SHELLEY TAYLOR-SMITH

FOR MARATHON SWIMMER SHELLEY TAYLOR-SMITH, THE CALL TO ADVENTURE CAME NOT AS A RESULT OF HER BRILLIANT SWIMMING CAREER, BUT AS THE RESULT OF A BRUSH WITH BREAST CANCER. FOLLOWING THE REMOVAL OF A MALIGNANT TUMOUR, TAYLOR-SMITH DEVELOPED A NEWFOUND LOVE FOR LIFE WHICH PLACED HER EXISTENCE IN PERSPECTIVE.

'Being world champion is not my number one priority now. It's not the be-all and end-all. Looking back I have to admit it meant more to me to be a world champion than to be a wife. Now it's not consuming me and I've never been so passionate about life.

I always wanted to motivate and inspire, to make a difference in this world. But I never knew how. Now I feel as though I'm on this earth for a reason and that I'm going to do my darnedest to help the youth of this country. They've just been lost for some reason. It's about our youth not worrying about whether they're wearing the right clothes, but about whether they're doing what they want to do. About individuality.'

In every film you watch and in every life you admire, people are called to adventure. It happens at different stages in their lives. For some, like Mother Teresa, the call becomes a life's work. For others, it may just represent a turning point or a significant stage in history which affects everybody around them. Whatever the case, the common thread emerges that your call to adventure will take you out of your ordinary world and into uncharted waters.

HERO

MARTIN LUTHER KING

'I HAVE A DREAM. IT IS A DREAM DEEPLY ROOTED IN THE AMERICAN DREAM.

I HAVE A DREAM THAT ONE DAY OUR NATION WILL RISE UP AND LIVE OUT THE TRUE MEANING OF ITS CREED – 'WE HOLD THESE TRUTHS TO BE SELF EVIDENT THAT ALL MEN ARE CREATED EQUAL.'

I HAVE A DREAM THAT ON THE RED HILLS OF GEORGIA, THE SONS OF FORMER SLAVES AND THE SONS OF FORMER SLAVE OWNERS WILL BE ABLE TO SIT AT THE TABLE OF BROTHERHOOD.

I HAVE A DREAM THAT ONE DAY, EVEN IN THE STATE OF MISSISSIPPI, A STATE SWELTERING FROM THE HEAT OF INJUSTICE, SWELTERING FROM THE HEAT OF OPPRESSION, WILL BE TRANSFORMED INTO AN OASIS OF FREEDOM AND JUSTICE.

I HAVE A DREAM THAT MY FOUR LITTLE CHILDREN WILL ONE DAY LIVE IN A NATION WHERE THEY WILL NOT BE JUDGED BY THE COLOUR OF THEIR SKIN BUT BY THE CONTENT OF THEIR CHARACTER. I HAVE A DREAM TODAY...'

AMERICAN CIVIL RIGHTS CAMPAIGNER MARTIN LUTHER KING GAVE PERHAPS THE GREATEST CALL TO ADVENTURE IN MODERN HISTORY IN HIS 'I HAVE A DREAM' ADDRESS IN 1964.

Despite the unfairness of the circumstances facing him and the enormous oppression of a system geared to bring about his downfall, Martin Luther King managed to inspire millions with his call to unite Americans against racism.

While the call to adventure often appears in the form of adversity or challenge, it sometimes appears in a very positive form. For example: a business opportunity, a new position of leadership, or winning an unexpected award. When life throws these gifts to you, make sure you appreciate them. Many people go through life too scared to have a great time. They keep putting things off until another day, when everything is perfect. The truth is, nothing is ever perfect. There are always reasons why you should or shouldn't go ahead with a project at a certain time. The same thing can be said of relationships. Many people spend their lives looking for the perfect partner only to discover there is no such thing. Instead there is only experience and as we know experiences, like people, have both their good and bad points. So, during your lifetime you may experience many different calls to adventure on many different levels. The key is to listen carefully to the messages and try to align them with who you are and what your purpose in life is.

'I'M GUIDED
BY MY HEART,
NOT MONEY
AND FAME.
IF YOU'RE NOT,
I RECKON YOU'RE
SCREWED UP.'
CATHY FREEMAN CHAMPION ATHLETE

LISTEN FOR THE RIGHT CALL

One of the key components in answering your call to adventure is learning to surrender to the real message. Great speakers like Martin Luther King and Nelson Mandela have inspired so many because their words hit home in people's hearts.

WHAT IS YOUR PURPOSE?

The question is now **What is your purpose?** And where does school fit into this? The answers to these questions do not come easily, but they do come! **We believe that every single person is born with a unique gift and that your journey in life is to discover that gift and to learn how to share it with others.**

Most people never really discover their calling in life, because they are too 'comfortable' in mediocrity; taking their gifts for granted so much they never even begin to use them to their full potential.

Many people have been so conditioned into mediocrity that they refuse to hear the call when it comes. Even on the smallest of scales, people refuse to accept the journeys that lie in front of them. For example why is it you procrastinate so much before calling a potential boyfriend or girlfriend for the first time? Why is it you continue to put off doing homework or office work when you know it will help your career? Why is it every second person in the western world is going to go on a diet tomorrow and not today? The answer lies in the fact that to do these things means taking a risk. You might get rejected, you might fail, you might not lose weight! For many of us it is only when we are given no choice that we really get going on things. Magically, when this happens we often discover the person we thought we were is no match for the one we really are.

Q: WHAT IS STOPPING YOU RIGHT NOW FROM BEING THE PERSON YOU REALLY WANT TO BE?

A: NOTHING EXCEPT YOUR LIMITING BELIEFS.

Q:WHY SHOULDN'T YOU BE LEADING THE MOST COMPELLING, PASSIONATE, INSPIRING LIFE YOU CAN?

Q:WHY AREN'T YOU FULL OF ENERGY AND EXCITEMENT EVERY MORNING?

Q:WHY DOES LIFE SOMETIMES SEEM SO DARK?

A: BECAUSE IT'S EASIER TO BE MORBID AND DEPRESSED THAN TO SET YOURSELF GREAT CHALLENGES IN LIFE.

A PURPOSE IS NOT SOMETHING YOU CREATE, IT IS SOMETHING YOU DISCOVER.

With all this in mind it is important to accept that most journeys we begin never end where we thought they would. Journeys are designed to change you and, in the process, your expectations and dreams change as well. For this reason so long as you keep moving on your hero's journey and keep trying new things, you can't really fail because the real journey is only on the inside.

By this statement we mean that your purpose is something that already lies inside you. You do not have to go out to find that something – rather, you have to go in and find it. The only real way to achieve this is to start testing yourself in areas which challenge you.

When you link who you are with where you are going and tie them both to a purpose which really drives you, you will become unstoppable. We're not saying it will be easy work, but it will be an adventure.

Setting goals and detailing exactly the life you want to lead is an essential step in addressing your call to adventure. The key when setting goals is to start really big and then work backwards to the present moment, breaking the journey into achievable pieces.

> ‘I NOW BELIEVE THE LIFE WE LEAD ON EARTH IS BUT A MOSQUITO’S WING COMPARED TO THE ETERNITY AND THE LIFE HEREAFTER.’

HERO

MUHAMMAD ALI

WORLD HEAVYWEIGHT CHAMPION,1964-67, 1974-78

In a journey that has taken him from Olympic champion, to three times heavyweight champion of the world, to draft dodger, to black activist to a life hampered by Parkinson's disease, Muhammad Ali stands out as a man whose journey has taken on greater meaning outside the ring than it ever did during his brilliant career in it. In the introduction to the book, *Muhammad Ali: In Perspective*, Ali talks about his call to adventure.

‘As I've grown older I've become a more spiritual person than I was when I was young. I now believe the life we lead on earth is but a mosquito's wing compared to the eternity and the life hereafter. And I've learned that whatever time we spend here on Earth should be spent helping others and creating justice and equality for all people; not out of pity or shame, but out of love for all people with the knowledge that we belong not to many races but to one race — the human race…

And I hope that, like the Olympic flame, my life will light up the world with hope and love for all people. That to me is the true meaning of my life when I put it "into perspective".’

For Muhammad Ali, the hero's journey has always been about being true to himself. He has never been a person to allow public or popular opinion to sway his personal convictions. As a result, Ali has gone against society many times and also made a few enemies, but when he stood at the Olympic cauldron in Atlanta, his movements slow, his hands shaking from the effects of Parkinson's disease, he displayed an inner strength easily the equal of anything he ever achieved in the ring as a boxer. He showed us all that greatness is not something to be measured by Olympic medals or world championships, but rather by dignity and the strength of the human spirit.

'THE PURPOSE OF
LIFE IS TO SEEK
HAPPINESS.'
HIS HOLINESS THE DALAI LAMA

HOW TO MAP THE PROCESS OF YOUR JOURNEY

His Holiness the Dalai Lama makes the statement that the purpose of life is to seek happiness. The hero's journey is also about seeking happiness, but in order to do this it is important that you understand the difference between happiness and pleasure.

Many people make the mistake of confusing happiness and pleasure by assuming that happiness is easy to achieve. Happiness is very aligned with purpose, and as the lives of Martin Luther King, Muhammad Ali, Nelson Mandela and others have shown, sometimes pursuing your purpose can be enormously challenging.

The best way to distinguish between pleasure and happiness is to understand that pleasure is only ever short term. Pleasure is a quick fix, but does it really ever last? Happiness, however, endures almost anything. Happiness breeds resilience while pleasure breeds apathy.

Sometimes in your life you might be enduring terrible hardship on the road to living your dreams, but when asked the question are you happy, your heart sounds a resounding yes.

Goal setting can also lead you to aspire to things that will not make you happy, but unfortunately you often don't find this out until you arrive at the end. Money is a really good example of this. People who set making money as a goal rarely achieve happiness. The goal instead should be how you are going to spend your money. This gives you a greater motive for action and, so long as your goal is aligned with who you are and what you purpose is, you will eventually find happiness.

In this way we come to understand the old saying that it is not reaching your goals that is important: it is the person you become in the process.

‹EXIT

REFUSING THE CALL

LUCI 'S STORY

For many people, when the call to adventure comes, they are not ready to receive it. In most situations this results in escapism and denial. The following story by teenager Luci Kerr outlines how she refused to hear her early calls to adventure until she tried to take her life in a night that would be the turning point in her life.

'Once I wrote eight suicide letters in one night. I hadn't been to school for nine months, and I just couldn't see any light. Mum had mental illness at the time and I had nowhere to turn. I hated myself and I thought suicide was the only escape.

I even remember the night of 10 February. I sat up all night writing letters to my friends explaining why I was going to kill myself. I wrote a 32-page letter to my best friend and not a single word to my parents. They didn't deserve it. I just sat there listening to my favourite song, 'Bad for Good' by Take That, and wrote all night.

Next I chose a bridge over the freeway. It was stupid, but in my mind I was seeing the headlines next day in the paper. I suppose I was just trying to hope that in my death at least my life would amount to something.

On the way to the bridge, I posted all the letters. I can still remember walking up to the bridge so full of hate and at the same time feeling relief that at least it would all be over soon. I remember climbing up the stairs to the bridge and when I got to the top I didn't even hesitate: I just ran straight for the rail, pushed my hands onto it and jumped into the darkness.

Even now I can remember hitting the road and feeling really heavy as though I was sinking into it. I felt no pain, just waves of shock washing over me, like drugs. I tried to push myself up with my hands, but it was like I was stuck to the road… I couldn't believe I was still alive. I felt very peaceful and then I finally blacked out into nothing.

When I finally woke up in hospital I was really disappointed and angry with myself. Even though it was a miracle I survived, I still thought people would not believe I had wanted to kill myself. I was in intensive care for eleven days and all I can remember is my mum telling the nurses I was "just being silly" and my dad saying, "What are you going to do next, jump off a cliff?"

In many ways those words became my call to adventure. Even though my parents weren't much help, the nurses in that hospital were amazing. They helped me to realise that my number wasn't up and that I'd survived that fall for a reason. For the first time in my life, in that hospital, I felt I was surrounded by people who cared about me and that really gave me hope for the future.

THAT'S THE REAL IRONY ABOUT SUICIDE. NO ONE WANTS TO TALK TO YOU ABOUT IT UNTIL YOU'VE DONE IT. THEN THEY WON'T LEAVE YOU ALONE.

So my call to adventure taught me this. You just don't know what to expect in life and even when it seems hopeless there is always a way out, you just have to go and get help to find it. I really regret what I did. I gave up too easily and acted the victim all the time. When you think the world is against you, you feel very isolated; like no one understands you; until you get so depressed you can't find any reasons to go on.

So maybe the reason I survived is so others can learn from my story. Maybe that's my purpose. My next project is I'm going to write a book about my life. Hopefully it will help others in the same position I was in. I believe in fate, everything happens for a reason, I'm definitely meant to be here. There's so much more in life to do that I'm meant to do and refusing that call just takes me back where I started.'

LOOKING FOR EXCUSES

For many people this is as far as they ever get on the hero's journey. At the point when things start to get really hard, most people start looking for excuses to avoid the pain of having to go on with the journey.

There are many ways people refuse the call to adventure. Right now, the best way for you to avoid these excuses is to take the first step in your mind.

Before going onto Chapter 3, take the time to write out on a piece of paper exactly what you want to achieve in the following five areas of your life.

1. Personal success goals

2. School / Business / Work success goals

3. Leisure / Activity goals

4. Community goals

5. Spiritual balance goals

Once you have completed this for each of the five sections, break them down into achievable chunks, working backwards from the goal to the present moment.

When you have finished, look back over your goals and then ask yourself this key question: **What sort of person do I need to be to achieve these goals?**

If the goals mean enough to you, becoming the person you have always dreamed of being will happen during the process.

230

301

020

040

1 2 3 4 5.

EXCUSES AND ESCAPES

Life is full of people with hard luck stories about how they could have made it if …
Life is also full of people who sit back and watch the successful people and marvel at
how 'lucky' they are. They marvel at the great 'gifts' the talented were born with and
they marvel at the 'breaks ' that successful people seem to get.

In reality, most people who are successful got there because they worked hard at it.
They got there because they refused to accept excuses and no matter what happened
to them along the way, they never allowed themselves to give into the critics or to stop
trying to live their dream.

What many people choose to do is label themselves as 'hopeless' or 'unlucky' or
'unworthy' in order to avoid the real difficulty of setting out into the unknown. While
successful people may be lucky or gifted, they also have to show incredible faith in
themselves to get what they want in life. Entering the unknown never comes easily.

Most people never leave the comfort zone and set out into the unknown. Even when
the comfort zone becomes unbearable and their life is full of pain and disillusionment,
some people, still choose not to go on the hero's journey because they would rather
deal with their life of escapes and excuses than have to face the fear of setting out
on an adventure with an unknown outcome.

Drug addiction is a classic example of this. Many drug addicts are driven to drugs
because of the inclusive culture which initially surrounds taking drugs. By taking
drugs they choose to escape the uncertainty of having to discover who they really
are and replace this with the instant gratification drugs initially bring. As time wears
on, the escape becomes the excuse. 'I can't live my dreams… I 'm a drug addict.'

It is here the hero's journey becomes difficult. To take the hero's journey you often
have to take the road less travelled. This means avoiding excuses and escapes even
when things happen which are so unfair, giving up seems to be the only option. It is
in moving through these moments that you begin to discover that the person you
thought you were is no match for the one you really are.

'I PREFER ENGAGING IN LIFE RATHER THAN OBSERVING IT. GET INVOLVED! GET IT ALL OVER YOU! PEOPLE GET SO EXASPERATED WITH LIFE. THEY WON'T LET THINGS JUST HAPPEN.'
RUSSELL CROWE

HERO
RUSSELL CROWE

Actor Russell Crowe's journey started in New Zealand in 1964. After moving to Australia and taking small roles as a child actor, he managed to move through some very hard times and emerge against the odds to become one of Hollywood's biggest stars.

But far from getting caught up in all the hype, Russell has managed to keep his feet on the ground. Often seen at his farm in New South Wales or supporting his favourite rugby side, the South Sydney Rabbitohs, Russell Crowe's journey is inspiring because he does not seem to have lost a sense of himself despite the enormous media attention which constantly follows him around.

While many would look at Russell Crowe's life and say he is lucky, at some stage he was just another ordinary bloke with a dream to become an actor. What separates him from the rest may well be talent and luck but above all it is the courage to have a real go at things.

'I CAN'T BE DISPASSIONATELY REMOVED FROM THE THINGS I DO. I REALLY FEEL SORRY FOR PEOPLE WHO ARE, WHO DIVIDE THEIR WHOLE LIFE UP INTO "THINGS THAT I LIKE" AND "THINGS THAT I MUST DO." YOU'RE ONLY HERE FOR A SHORT TIME, MATE – LEARN TO LIKE IT.'

The films *Braveheart* and *Dangerous Minds* offer us an insight into how people often accept or reject the call to adventure.

'EVERY MAN DIES, BUT NOT EVERY MAN TRULY LIVES.'

WILLIAM WALLACE 'BRAVEHEART'

FILM
BRAVEHEART

Braveheart is an epic set in thirteenth century Scotland. Based around the true story of legendary Scotsman William Wallace, the film plots the rise and fall of Wallace as he gathers the Scottish tribes to free his country from the tyrannical reign of the English king, Edward Longshanks.

Wallace's call to adventure begins when the English brutally murder his wife. Initially driven by revenge, Wallace begins to discover his real purpose is to unite the clans against the English and claim freedom for Scotland.

Prior to the death of his wife, Wallace wanted nothing more than a peaceful life as a farmer. However, when life deals him the unfairest of blows and takes his wife, Wallace is faced with a call to adventure he cannot ignore. Once he had claimed his revenge, however, Wallace was faced with the choice of either returning to life as a simple farmer or leading his people to oust the English completely from the country.

It was at this moment that Wallace had to decide. Do I carry on in a quest for freedom, or do I return to the safety of an ordinary life?

You will receive many such calls in your own life and the only way to find the answer is to know yourself well enough to listen to the voice of your spirit. For William Wallace, this came easily and he decided to press on and eventually ended up invading England. For the rest of us, however, this process is often harder to begin. Knowing who you are and being able to listen to yourself in times of difficulty takes great courage and understanding.

Watch *Braveheart* and see if you can identify the stages of the hero's journey.

ORDINARY WORLD *Following the brutal death of his family at the hands of the English, William Wallace was raised by his uncle on the European mainland and returned to Scotland to marry his childhood sweetheart.*

CALL TO ADVENTURE *Wallace's call to adventure came following the murder of his wife. After leading the clans to victory Wallace was then faced with another call to unite the clans and invade England.*

TESTS *Wallace's test came through the physical battles with the English. He also had to face the lack of loyalty from his own followers and had to let go of the pain caused by his wife's death.*

ENEMIES *The king of England, Edward Longshanks, the clan leaders and on occasions, Robert the Bruce.*

ALLIES *Wallace's allies came in the form of his uncle and his wife. Wallace also won the heart of the king's daughter-in-law and his army remained loyal to the end.*

SLAYING THE DRAGON *For Wallace the dragon had a number of forms. Firstly he had to overcome the death of his wife and finally he had to accept that although he had been betrayed many times in his struggle, he would refuse to swear allegiance to the king, even though this meant dying a horrible death.*

REWARD *In the end, Wallace's reward was knowing that he had remained true to himself and the ideal of freedom he held so strongly. Despite his death, his legacy lived on and his life inspired the Scottish to eventually unite under Robert the Bruce at Bannockburn in 1314 and win back their freedom.*

It was only through adversity that William Wallace discovered his real purpose in life. Very often the most remarkable human achievements emerge from the worst possible situations. It would be a good thing to keep this in mind next time you have a major problem in your life. Don't be one of the many who get so caught up in self-pity that they miss the opportunities life has to offer.

'THERE ARE NO VICTIMS IN THIS CLASSROOM.'

FILM
DANGEROUS MINDS

Dangerous Minds is a film about a former marine, Louanne Johnson, who follows her dream to become a teacher. In the process Louanne finds herself teaching a group of inner-city teenagers who have come to accept failure as a way of life. Determined to earn their respect and make a difference in their lives, Louanne becomes emotionally involved with her students and sets out to 'save them from themselves.'

Louanne's call to adventure comes on her first teaching day, when the students reject her efforts leaving her feeling humiliated and disillusioned. Louanne is now faced with the big question: does she give up her efforts to make a difference in the lives of her students and go to an easier job, or does she stay and try to overcome the circumstances even though no-one believes in her.

Louanne's choice to stay is a decision to face one of the most difficult obstacles on the hero's journey. To stay means facing the critics and putting yourself on the line. It means being prepared to fail.

How do you react in situations such as this? Having missed a shot to win a basketball game one week, would you call for the ball the next week in the same position? Having asked a person to go out with you and then being rejected would you have the strength to keep faith in yourself and go and ask someone else the next time? These are the types of questions we have to regularly answer in life. They are often great leaning experiences but the learning is only valuable if you use the experience to grow. For many, the first rejection is often the last and they spend their lives avoiding rejection rather than seeking to be themselves.

Watch *Dangerous Minds* and see if you can identify the stages of the hero's journey.

ORDINARY WORLD *Rejected by her husband and unemployed, Louanne Johnson wants to become a teacher.*

CALL TO ADVENTURE *When a job comes up at a tough inner-city high school, Louanne applies for the position, only to discover she has been given the worst class in the school.*

TESTS *Rejected by the students and unsupported by the school's principal, Louannne has to decide whether she is going to stay on at the school. Having made the decision and managed to get her students onside, Louanne then has to deal with the death of a student (Emilio) in a gang-related murder.*

ALLIES *During her ordeal, Louanne relies on her close friend who is also a teacher. But above all it is her students who recognise her talent and support her in her hours of need.*

SLAYING THE DRAGON *Louanne takes the death of the student very personally. Having tried to steer him away from the deadly confrontation with local gang members, Louanne feels responsible and hopeless when Emilio is killed. As a result she decides to leave the school feeling that she has not been able to make any difference.*

REWARD *When Louanne tells her class she has resigned, they convince her to stay by quoting her own words back to her. Slowly Louanne realises that she had been making a difference in her students' lives and more importantly that she had been making a difference in her own. By choosing to stay at the school despite Emilio's death, she is showing herself and her students that she can make a difference, no matter what the circumstances.*

SUMMARY
THE CALL TO ADVENTURE

LIVE LIFE WITHOUT REGRETS AND VALUE THOSE CLOSE TO YOU.

MANY PEOPLE WHO HAVE ACCOMPLISHED GREAT THINGS IN THEIR LIVES, HAVE DONE SO NOT IN SPITE OF SERIOUS SETBACKS, BUT BECAUSE OF THEM.

THE CALL TO ADVENTURE WILL COME TO YOU IN MANY DISGUISES, MANY TIMES OVER.

A PURPOSE IS NOT SOMETHING YOU CREATE, BUT SOMETHING YOU DISCOVER. IT EMERGES AS AN EXPRESSION OF SELF.

YOUR REAL POWER LIES IN WHO YOU ARE.

SETTING GOALS IS A KEY STEP TO REACHING THE DESTINATION

EVERYONE IS BORN WITH A GIFT; YOUR JOURNEY IS TO DISCOVER IT.

CHAPTER 3
THE SPECIAL WORLD

It is not the critic who counts,
not the one who points out how the strong one stumbles
or where the doer of deeds could have done them better.
The credit belongs to the one who is actually in the arena,
whose face is marred by dust and sweat and blood,
who strives valiantly,
who errs and comes up short again and again
because there is no effort without error or shortcomings,
who knows great devotion,
who spends themselves in a worthy cause,
who at best knows in the end
knows the high achievement of triumph
and who at worst, if they fail while daring greatly,
knows their place shall never be with those timid and cold souls
who know neither victory nor defeat.

THEODORE ROOSEVELT TWENTY-SIXTH PRESIDENT OF THE USA

UPON ENTERING THE SPECIAL WORLD, THERE IS NO TURNING BACK. IF YOU HAVE ACCEPTED RESPONSIBILITY FOR YOUR JOURNEY AND YOU UNDERSTAND YOUR PURPOSE, THIS IS AN EXCITING TIME. HOWEVER, AS THE JOURNEY MOVES FORWARD, AND BECOMES MORE DIFFICULT, YOU REALISE THE REAL JOURNEY IS TAKING PLACE INSIDE YOURSELF. THE BATTLE TO ACCEPT RESPONSIBILITY AND NOT TO JUSTIFY, LAY BLAME OR DENY WHAT IS HAPPENING TO YOU IS THE REAL HURDLE. NO MATTER WHETHER YOUR SPECIAL WORLD IS A POSITIVE OR NEGATIVE ENVIRONMENT, THE LESSON WHICH EMERGES IS CLEAR. IF YOU ARE TO MOVE FORWARD, YOU MUST ACCEPT THAT YOUR DESTINY IS IN YOUR OWN HANDS. OFTEN YOU WILL NEED A MENTOR TO HELP YOU SEE THIS FOR YOURSELF.

EVERY JOURNEY BEGINS WITH A SINGLE STEP

As Jesse Martin's story told us (see page 17), the courage required to leave your comfort zone and set out on any journey is enormous. Not only do you have to be strong enough to handle the critics, but you also need belief in yourself to keep going even when you doubt yourself. For these and other reasons, many people only ever dream of attempting an adventure in life but never get around to taking the first step. Instead they fill their lives with excuses designed to avoid the reality of actually setting out.

Ironically, it is only once you have started the journey that you begin to realise starting is often the hardest part. Journeys help us to grow, they help us to refine and develop the courage, strength and knowledge which makes even greater adventures possible.

So, once you have established what your special world is, take the first step!

Know who you are

Live your DREAMS

start your
journey
NOW

FIND YOUR SPIRIT

THE SPECIAL WORLD IS BOTH A POSITIVE AND NEGATIVE PLACE

What people fear most about the special world is that it often exposes their major character flaws. If you choose not to learn from this, you will find you keep failing at exactly the same place each time. In fact, some people even set themselves up to fail to avoid having to overcome a fundamental flaw, even though they know this is the only way to move forward in the journey.

Many people even avoid going on journeys because they are not too sure where it is they want to go or what it is they want to do. They procrastinate so much they never go anywhere. They are filled with the fear that this may not be the journey for them. In the end, however, which journey you start on is not really important. So long as you remain adaptable, the wrong journey can be a great learning experience. It can often help you define what the right journey is. So long as you remain honest and accept that failure and wrong decisions are nothing more than stepping stones to success and the right decisions, you can't fail.

HARLEY'S STORY

The following story from Harley Walker outlines how difficult it can be to live in the special world when you're not honest about why you are there.

'A few years ago, I entered a really negative special world. It was the world of drugs, gangs and graffiti. The idea was just to run with the biggest crew and do the most damage you could to anything, including yourself.

I did everything in those early years, drugs, sedatives, the lot, and for a while it was great. I was a part of something. It was a special world but in my heart I knew I was there for all the wrong reasons. My dad was a school teacher at my school and I really rebelled against that.

My special world was a school gang which I thought gave me respect. Suddenly being in the gang, it didn't matter what other people thought of me. I was a part of something big, but as the years went on, I never really developed. I wasn't honest with myself.

If I was honest with myself, I would have seen that the special gang world was not that special at all. One night we rolled this old lady and sprayed her with graffiti paint. For me that was turning point. I couldn't believe what I had done to be part of this special gang world. It even makes me sick to talk about it now. I can remember walking away with the others laughing, but inside I was sick at what we had done.

So for me, that was my entry into the special world. I had to be honest with myself and just admit the only reason I was in that gang was I was too afraid to stand on my own.

That's when I discovered my music. For me now pursuing a career in music is my special world. Believing I was good enough was the real hurdle I had to overcome. I'd been told so many times I was useless, I had started to believe it.

When I left the gang to pursue my music career, I was addicted to drugs and had no other friends. It was the hardest time of my life. But that's what the special world is about sometimes, you have to overcome these things that were holding you back all the time. I fell over now and then, but the best part was I felt at least now I was controlling my life.

I know now in life I am going to amount to something. I am going to be something special. I want to touch people and share my message. I am surrounding myself with people who believe in me and not with ones who always want to cut you down.

The journey won't be easy but at least it will be mine.'

ACCEPT OR REJECT THE JOURNEY

Like Harley, you will find you have many false starts on your journey. If you read the biographies of anyone who has achieved great things in their life, you'll see they failed many times before they succeeded. The key to the first step is accepting responsibility for the journey.

In Chapter 5 you will read about US President Abraham Lincoln who failed eleven times before eventually becoming president of the United States. Many people spend a lifetime searching for the right journey. They are always starting journeys but never finishing them. Sometimes not finishing a journey is a good move.

For example, mountaineer Jim Hayhurst, tells the story of his attempt to climb Mount Everest. He and his crew got so close to the summit they could see it and then one by one they began to turn back. In the end, after climbing more than nine-tenths of the way to the top, the final crew members turned back. The expedition had cost tens of thousands of dollars and taken years to prepare and not one of the climbers had made it to the top. When asked if the journey had been a success, Hayhurst replied, 'Personally and as a team we felt successful. We all had done our personal bests… We all lived. And we learned, individually and collectively. I learned about core values. I learned about choosing the right mountain.'

What Hayhurst is saying is that the only person with the right to judge your journey is you and as long as you have given your best, you should feel comfortable judging it as a success.

'WHAT IS THE DEFINITION OF SUCCESS? TRUE SUCCESS IS THE ATTAINMENT OF PURPOSE WITHOUT COMPROMISING CORE VALUES.'
JIM HAYHURST

NOT EVERYTHING THAT HAPPENS TO YOU IS YOUR FAULT; BUT IT BECOMES YOUR RESPONSIBILITY.

IT'S NOT WHETHER YOU WIN OR LOSE BUT WHAT YOU LEARN IN THE PROCESS THAT SEPARATES THE WINNERS AND THE LOSERS.

ACCEPTING RESPONSIBILITY

SUCCESSFUL PEOPLE, NO MATTER WHAT FIELD OF EXPERTISE THEY ARE IN, OR HOW DIFFERENT THEY MAY BE FROM EACH OTHER, ALL HAVE ONE THING IN COMMON – THEY HAVE LEARNED TO ACCEPT RESPONSIBILITY FOR THEIR CIRCUMSTANCES.

Whether it be in sport, in art, or in anything else, they have learned to look further than the scoreboard, the critic's review, or the opinions of others.

People who take responsibility actually look within themselves for the answers. They accept the full responsibility each time they 'fail' because they know that in doing so, they learn how to do it better next time. So the next time you get beaten on the scoreboard, look at yourself as a learner, not a loser.

The real losers in this life are the ones who, instead of learning from their mistakes, choose to blame others and so never allow themselves to develop. They use a whole range of techniques to do this, including those listed below.

Here are four very common sporting excuses:

JUSTIFICATION *'Who cares? It was only a game and we'll beat them next time.'*

DENIAL *A week after the game you tell someone you played really well when, deep inside, you know you played a shocker.*

LAYING BLAME *'It wasn't my fault. It was my team-mates' fault. They're useless.'*

QUITTING *You give up early or fake an injury because in your heart you know you're going to lose anyway.*

Sound familiar? Well, take heart – we all use excuses from time to time to save ourselves actually having to accept responsibility for our actions. Sometimes it's neither here nor there, but other times to cop out is to rule yourself out of a promising future.

By not accepting the truth about a situation, you can never really understand why you failed and thus you can never understand how to succeed the next time. But in order to accept the truth you have to learn to be honest with yourself. You must start now. Every time you are faced with a difficult decision you have to ask if your chosen answer is honest.

To test this honesty make a list of all the bad things that have happened to you in your life. If you write them out chronologically and take a really hard look at them, you will see a pattern start to emerge. At the route of all these troubles one or two shining examples of 'dishonesty' will emerge.

More often than not, these examples of dishonesty will be the result of learned behaviours from your past. People who claim to have 'uncontrollable tempers' or 'genetic forgetfulness' are not really being honest. These are learned habits and therefore they can be unlearned. This process is not easy, but it is possible no matter what situation you are in.

Here's how.

1 Make a decision about the type of person you want to be in life.

2 Start being that person.

3 Make a decision about where you want to go in life.

4 Start going there.

5 Work out your fundamental weaknesses.

6 Start asking new questions that help you remove these weaknesses.

7 Start enjoying both failures and the successes of the hero's journey because if you remain honest they will both lead you to the same place.

WHEN YOUR PURPOSE IS THE PURPOSE OF YOUR SPIRIT, IT BECOMES ALMOST IMPOSSIBLE TO FIND EXCUSES.

HERO

LOUISE SAUVAGE

CONSIDER THE STORY OF WHEELCHAIR ATHLETE, LOUISE SAUVAGE. BORN WITH A SPINAL CONDITION KNOWN AS MYELODISPLASIA, LOUISE SPENT MUCH OF HER TEENAGE LIFE IN HOSPITALS HAVING METAL RODS SURGICALLY INSERTED INTO HER SPINE. IT TOOK HER OVER TWO YEARS TO RECOVER, AFTER WHICH TIME SHE TOOK UP SWIMMING AND TRACK AND ROAD RACING.

It would have been easy for Louise to drop her bundle and give up on life, to claim to be one of the victims. Instead she turned her misfortune into success. As an athlete she never laid blame on others or tried to justify quitting because of her spinal condition.

Her achievements are almost too many to list, but they include world championships, Olympic gold medals and world records. Suffice to say that if Louise Sauvage had won gold medals in the same events at the Barcelona and Sydney Olympics, as she did at the Paralympics, she would certainly be regarded as our greatest-ever athlete!

RESPONSIBILITY *EQUALS*

LEARNING TO ACCEPT RESPONSIBILITY

EACH TIME SOMETHING ON YOUR HERO'S JOURNEY DOESN'T TURN OUT THE WAY YOU PLANNED IT, ASK YOURSELF WHY? COULD IT BE ONE OF THOSE LIMITING BELIEFS WE DISCUSSED BACK IN CHAPTER 1? COULD IT BE THAT YOU ARE JUST SCARED TO LEAVE YOUR COMFORT ZONE?

The key to this section of the hero's journey is learning to **accept responsibility for your own actions and their consequences**. In order to change our circumstances, we must first learn to acknowledge them and to accept that, no matter how unfair they may seem, life is not always fair. This is really hard for some people to accept, but once you do accept it, coping with failure and bad luck becomes easier.

So what does the word responsibility actually mean? It means a person's ability to **respond** in a given situation. People who show little responsibility in their lives tend to be those who are always **reacting** to life: they lose their cool and act rashly. Those who pause for a moment when they are challenged, and think before they make their next move, are responding to life.

A reaction is an emotional impulse to a set of circumstances. Reactions are often rash and undisciplined and more inclined to be ego-driven than driven by the spirit.

Responses, however, require you to temper your reaction with some thought. They require discipline and self-understanding and they are ten times more productive than reactions.

If you respond to all the challenges in your life and give them your best shot, you can't fail. It is only when you avoid the truth that you fail. Most people go on the hero's journey expecting certain outcomes and inevitably they are disappointed when those outcomes are not achieved. In the journey of relationships, for example, most young people tend to go into them with the romantic view that they will always be as passionately in love with their partner as they were when they first started going out. By setting this expectation, you are doing nothing more than ensuring the failure of the relationship. People and relationships grow and change and so will you on your journey. So in order to respond, as you grow, you must be open to change. You must be open to respond to life as it deals you the cards, and not react to life when it doesn't deal you the cards you think you deserve.

ABILITY TO RESPOND

LAYING BLAME

IN HIS BOOK, AWAKEN THE GIANT WITHIN, *ANTHONY ROBBINS TOLD THE STORY OF AN AMERICAN GUY WHO WAS SERVING A LIFE SENTENCE IN PRISON FOR MULTIPLE MURDER. THIS MAN HAD TWO SONS. MANY YEARS INTO HIS PRISON SENTENCE, HIS TWO SONS WERE FOLLOWED UP TO SEE WHAT HAD BECOME OF THEM. IT DIDN'T TAKE LONG TO TRACK THEM DOWN.*

Ironically, the first son was now also serving a life sentence for murder and so they asked him why he thought he'd turned out like that? He answered, 'What would you expect with a father like mine?'

The other son had become a successful businessman and was happily married with two kids. When he was asked why he thought he'd turned out like that, he also answered, 'What would you expect with a father like mine?'

Why did two brothers with the same past turn out so differently? At one time or another we have all blamed someone else for the situation in which we find ourselves.

Write down a time you avoided responsibility for your actions by blaming someone else.

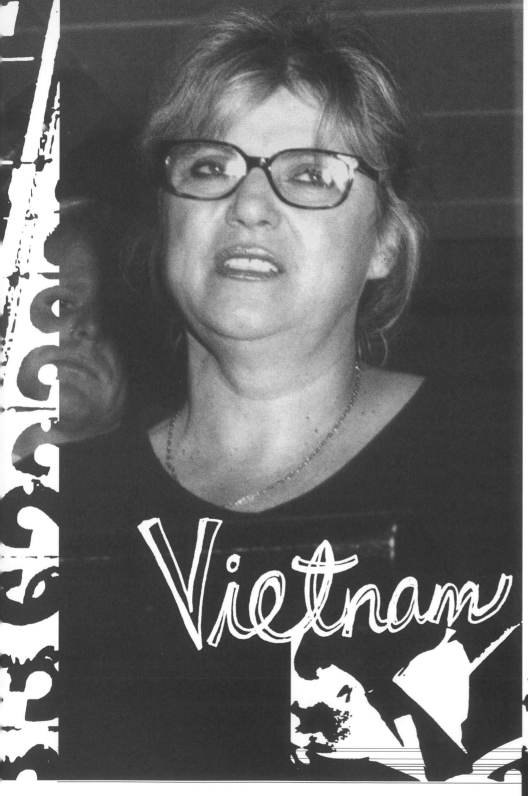

Vietnam

HERO
CHRISTINA NOBLE

CHRISTINA NOBLE WAS BORN IN THE SLUMS OF DUBLIN, IRELAND IN 1944. ONE OF THREE SIBLINGS SHE WAS RAISED BY HER MOTHER AND HER ALCOHOLIC FATHER. AT THE AGE OF TEN, CHRISTINA'S MOTHER DIED AND THE CHILDREN WERE SEPARATED AND SENT TO ORPHANAGES. CHRISTINA SPENT FOUR DESPERATE YEARS IN AN INSTITUTION BELIEVING THAT HER BROTHERS AND SISTERS WERE DEAD. HER EVENTUAL ESCAPE BROUGHT HER TO PHOENIX PARK IN DUBLIN WHERE SHE SLEPT IN A HOLE IN THE GROUND THAT SHE DUG HERSELF. IT WAS DURING THIS VULNERABLE TIME THAT CHRISTINA WAS SUBJECTED TO A GANG RAPE AND BECAME PREGNANT. A BABY BOY WAS BORN BUT TAKEN FOR ADOPTION AGAINST HER WILL.

At the age of 18 Christina ran away to England to be with her brother. This is where she met and married her husband and had three children, Helenita, Nicolas and Androula. Unfortunately the cycle of abuse continued as her husband proved himself to be a violent and unfaithful man. She was regularly beaten, suffered a miscarriage and was later forced to undertake shock treatment for a mental breakdown and depression. It was during this particularly low ebb in her life around 1971 that she had a dream about Vietnam.

'I don't know why I dreamed about Vietnam, perhaps it was because the country was so much in the news at the time. In the dream, naked Vietnamese children were running down a dirt road fleeing from a napalm bombing. The ground under the children was cracked and coming apart and the children were reaching to me. One of the girls had a look in her eyes that implored me to pick her up and protect her and take her to safety. Above the escaping children was a brilliant white light that contained the word Vietnam.'

This was a dream which Christina would one day triumphantly fulfil, albeit twenty years later. In 1989, with the goal to assist children in need, Christina arrived in Vietnam. Christina's story of courage is an inspiring example of someone who was prepared to risk everything to enter a special world where she now dedicates her efforts to helping street kids. As you can see from this story, Christina's motivation goes back into her own past. Rather than become a victim of the things which happened to her, Christina had the strength to rise above them and use her past as an inspiration to create a better future both for herself and others around her.

INSTEAD OF MAKING EXCUSES, START MAKING GOOD DECISIONS. CONSULT THOSE WHO HAVE GONE BEFORE YOU.

MAKING EXCUSES

ONE OF THE HARDEST TEMPTATIONS YOU WILL HAVE TO RESIST ON YOUR HERO'S JOURNEY IS CHOOSING TO MAKE UP AN EXCUSE TO AVOID ACCEPTING RESPONSIBILITY FOR YOUR SITUATION.

Spend next Saturday watching a local netball game. The chances are, if you stay there long enough, you will hear every player on the losing side walk off the court giving an excuse as to why they were beaten.

'My opponent was too rough.'

'She played dirty!'

'Did you hear what she said!'

'She was such a bitch!'

'The umpires were all on their side.'

'The sun was in my eyes.'

'I sprained my ankle.'

'I wasn't feeling well.'

And we could go on forever. Funnily enough, the one thing you almost certainly won't hear is the truth: 'I missed some really easy shots!'

The sad thing is, for as long as you don't acknowledge your weakness, you will never be able to improve in that area. In fact, if the hero's journey does anything, it exposes your weaknesses so you can learn from them. In the end they become your greatest ally on the journey.

Instead of making excuses, start making good decisions. Consult those who have gone before you. Try to use all you own experiences so that each failure becomes a learning tool. Try to use everything you have been given in life to help on your journey and accept that, while some are given more talent than others, we all have a special gift we can share with the world.

1 *The hero's journey is a choice.*

2 *The hardest part of that choice is accepting responsibility and taking the first step.*

3 *Once you are on the journey, you will need to make many choices and the more honest your choices the more your journey will grow.*

4 *Each failure on the hero's journey is a step closer to success.*

5 *The hero's journey takes determination, flexibility and courage. It will not be easy.*

6 *Learn to enjoy the journey with all its anxious moments of uncertainty, fluctuations in confidence and draining physical exhaustion because, as Albert Einstein once noted, 'the final emergence into the light' is the most satisfying moment a human can know and 'only those who have experienced it can understand it.'*

OUR GREATEST WEAKNESS LIES IN GIVING UP. THE MOST CERTAIN WAY TO SUCCEED IS ALWAYS TO TRY JUST ONE MORE TIME.

QUITTING

Learning the difference between quitting and changing direction is a very important lesson. A quitter is somebody who gives up and refuses to learn from their experiences. Somebody who changes direction, however, has acknowledged that the original path they chose was not quite leading them where they wanted to go. They had to change direction, while never forgetting that there was somewhere they did want to go.

Many of the great painters make hundreds of attempts before they manage to paint their masterpiece. All the same, if you were to line up all those 'failed attempts' in a row, you would see that the painter has neither quit nor failed – rather, they have learned from their mistakes and changed direction.

PARENTS ARE YOUR RESPONSIBILITY

Remember the brother who ended up in jail in the story on page 79? He blamed his father for the way he turned out. But whose responsibility was it really? **The fact is, no parents are perfect. Like all of us, they make mistakes**. But rather than blaming their mistakes for our failures, wouldn't it be better if we accepted responsibility for our own lives? Isn't it interesting how people who are happy and successful owe all of it to their parents, whereas those who are miserable and lack self-worth tend to blame their parents.

You do not have to be a victim of your family circumstances.

The film *Dragon* is the story of Bruce Lee, who has been confronted throughout his life by inner demons. After his father's death, Lee's mentor explains to him what these demons represent. 'They are your inner fears and they have been passed down to you by your father – and if you don't confront them you will pass them on to your children.'

At a recent workshop, the topic of fathers came up, and the role they need to play in the family and one girl made a profound statement. She said, 'Even though my father has lived with me for my sixteen years, he hasn't been there for fifteen.' Her father had a drinking problem and is unemployed and she had big issues with this. She found it difficult to love him and expected him to change. She wanted him to be like other fathers.

In the last six months, however, all this has changed, so that now she loves and respects him. So what happened? Her father hasn't changed. What have changed are her expectations. After going on her own inner journey, she realised her father was expressing his love for her by doing the best he could as a father. Until then, she had wanted to be loved on her terms, but when she let those terms go and was prepared to accept her father, warts and all, her heart opened.

FOR THINGS TO CHANGE, FIRST I MUST CHANGE.

As a step along the way of the hero's journey, write two letters. One to each parent, even if, for whatever reason, you never see them.

The purpose of these letters is to write down how you feel about these two people, without whom you would not exist. Write it from the heart, describing the good and the bad, if that's how you feel. Take your time and write your letters as though no-one will ever read them except you.

When you have finished the exercise, it is up to you to decide what to do with the letters. In our experience, some people ask each of their parents to write them a letter, and then they make an exchange; others throw their letters away, or burn them and let any resentment they have dissipate with them. Still others store them until a more fitting time.

Remember there is no right or wrong way along your path, each road is there for a reason, each one is there to teach us something. However, we are confident that most people will learn something very powerful from doing this exercise.

IT TAKES COURAGE TO ACKNOWLEDGE HOW YOU FEEL.

HERO
IAN THORPE

IAN THORPE'S JOURNEY INTO THE SPECIAL WORLD CAME AT A VERY YOUNG AGE. AT JUST FOURTEEN, IAN BECAME THE YOUNGEST EVER MALE SWIMMER TO BE NAMED IN THE AUSTRALIAN TEAM.

Ian has gone on to establish himself as one of the greatest swimmers of all time. Having broken numer-ous world records and won three Olympic gold and two silver medals, Ian has become a role model for young Australians.

Perhaps what is most impressive, however, is the fact that Ian has managed to develop his swimming career while not losing touch with other areas of his life. Despite participating in the special world of an international celebrity, Ian has also managed to become one of the most sought-after people in the world to advertise products and events.

Despite the apparent glamorous life, Ian's special world comes at a price. His training starts at 5am five mornings a week. Training lasts for two hours and then two days a week he backs this up with an hour of weight training. In the afternoons, Ian swims again for two hours and has only Wednesday mornings and Sundays off.

The special world you choose for yourself will always come at a price. The special world is never easy and long-term dedication is required to make it through.

AS AN INTERNATIONAL DIPLOMAT FOR PEACE AND LOVE, DIANA FOUND HER TRUE CALLING IN HELPING PEOPLE.

'IF I SHOULD DIE AND LEAVE YOU HERE A WHILE, BE NOT LIKE OTHERS, SORE UNDONE, WHO KEEP LONG VIGILS BY THE SILENT DUST AND WEEP.

FOR MY SAKE – TURN AGAIN TO LIFE AND SMILE, NERVING THY HEART AND TREMBLING HAND TO DO SOMETHING TO COMFORT OTHER HEARTS THAN THINE.

COMPLETE THOSE DEAR UNFINISHED TASKS OF MINE AND I PERCHANCE, MAY HEREIN COMFORT YOU.'

READ BY DIANA'S SISTER AT HER FUNERAL

HERO

LADY DIANA SPENCER

THE STORY OF LADY DIANA SPENCER IS A HERO'S JOURNEY OF A DIFFERENT KIND. SHE WAS A PRESCHOOL TEACHER IN NORTH LONDON WHO WAS THRUST INTO THE SPOTLIGHT TO BECOME THE MOST RECOGNISED PUBLIC FIGURE IN THE WORLD. DIANA SPENCER'S CALL TO ADVENTURE CHANGED HER LIFE FOREVER. AND YET, AS THE STORY UNFOLDED, IT BECAME APPARENT THAT HER TRUE CALL WAS YET TO COME.

Following her separation from Prince Charles, Diana adopted a new role, which was to earn her hero status in the hearts of millions of people around the world. As an international diplomat for peace and love, Diana found her true calling in helping people.

The message for the rest of the world was clear. As a princess, living a life that someone else had mapped out for her, Diana's life was out of balance. She developed an eating disorder, became extremely depressed and it is rumoured she may even have attempted suicide.

And so it was not surprising that following her tragic death in 1997, the world grieved her loss not as a princess, but as a person who tried to bring happiness and peace to those in need – a person who had listened and acted when her call had come. Like Muhammad Ali, Diana's power did not lie in the trappings that made her famous.

It lay instead in the smile and warmth that came from her spirit. In the future, history will not remember her as the Princess of Wales or a member of the royal family; but as the mother of her children and a helper of the poor, whose real power lay in the spirit of who she was and not in the myth of what she was.

FINDING
A MENTOR

For many people, the special world is a place where they find a mentor. Mentors are often people who have been through the experience you are about to embark on. The truer you are to yourself the more often mentors seem to appear.

Behind every success story is either a coach, parent, teacher or some person who is the hero's mentor. In film, it's often the wise old man or woman such as the Obi-Wan Kenobi in *Star Wars*, or even Robin Williams character in *Good Will Hunting*.

Mentors are those characters who teach and protect us in our early lives, and in doing so they share their wisdom, enabling us to fly.

If you have a dream in a certain area it is a very good idea to seek out someone who has already been where you want to go. You would be amazed how many people are out there doing great things who are willing to help.

Don't just rely on celebrities to be your role models. Actually, ninety-nine out of a hundred times, you will discover your real mentor turns out to be someone you have never heard of, someone who will hold the key that unlocks the door to your dreams.

You can have many mentors in your life, each doing their little bit, guiding, teaching and often pushing you towards self-discovery. Some are there to catch you as you fall, others to pick you up. Life has a way of guiding these people into your lives, but if you're preoccupied all the time you won't even know they are there.

YOUR DESTINY IS IN YOUR OWN HANDS

The bottom line here is that we all have dreams but not all of us have the courage and support to follow them. We all know that inside us there is a person waiting to emerge and live the life of our dreams, but still many of us choose not the hear that call. The longer you refuse to enter the special world and go on the journey the more difficult it becomes to contact the person inside.

Accepting that you have control over your own destiny is a vital step in the hero's journey. Many people find this hard to accept. They say, 'What if I get sick tomorrow?' 'What if I get hit by a bus?' 'What if I go broke trying to follow my dreams?'

Of course, one or all of these things may happen to you. The question to ask is this: will following my dreams make these events any more likely to occur? If the answer is yes, ask yourself whether itis worth the risk. If the answer is no, get another dream.

Life is not always fair and the special world is one of the least fair places you can ever travel through. But the rewards are always worthwhile. So instead of finding excuses for not starting the journey, stop waiting for the things around you to change and start changing yourself. Be honest and seek help in the process but remember the first step to changing anything, is changing yourself.

IT TAKES A WHOLE VILLAGE TO RAISE A CHILD.
AFRICAN PROVERB

'COME TO THE EDGE,' HE SAID.
THEY SAID, 'WE ARE AFRAID.'
'COME TO THE EDGE,' HE SAID. THEY CAME.
HE PUSHED THEM...AND THEY FLEW.'
GUILLAUME APOLLINAIRE FRENCH MAN OF LETTERS

'*MAKE EACH
DAY COUNT.*'

TITANIC

TITANIC IS THE LOVE STORY OF THE FREE-SPIRITED TRAVELLER, JACK, AND THE REPRESSED ARISTOCRATIC ROSE WHO FALL IN LOVE WHILE TRAVELLING ON THE TITANIC.

Rose is engaged to be married to a rich man named Cal who can look after her financially but is unable to give her the love and freedom she longs for. Feeling trapped and hopelessly lost in the social circle, Rose feels like her spirit is being crushed to the point where she considers committing suicide.

It is while attempting to jump from the back of the *Titanic* that Rose meets Jack, who not only saves her life but also introduces her to a special world of adventure and free-spirited love, which reawakens the passion in her soul. Just as Rose and Jack uncover the depth of their love for each other, the *Titanic* hits an iceberg and begins to sink.

It is here Rose's special new world of love will be put to the test. How much is she prepared to sacrifice for love? In the end Rose chooses to stay on board the sinking ship with Jack rather than be rowed to safety with the other first class passengers.

In doing so, she is both doomed and liberated at the same time. It is decisions such as this that are often required to take a journey through the special world. In Rose's case, she had to give up the comfort of married life in order to follow her dream of being with the man she really loved. She had to leap into the unknown with no guarantee of success.

This is often the hardest moment of the hero's journey because there are no certainties. It is all new ground.

Watch *Titanic* and see if you can follow Rose's journey.

ORDINARY WORLD *Rose's high-class aristocratic world of repression.*

CALL TO ADVENTURE *Rose meets Jack who tells her, 'If you jump, I jump.'*

SPECIAL WORLD *The Titanic and the world of love.*

ENEMIES *Cal, Rose's fiancé, and her mother.*

ALLIES *Jack and Molly.*

TESTS *Accepting Jack's note which asks her to 'Make each day count.'*

SLAYING THE DRAGON *Rose slays the dragon when she defies her mother and the society at large and jumps from the lifeboat to be with Jack on the sinking ship.*

REWARD *Although Jack dies in the end, he leaves Rose with the gift of knowing that she is worth much more than society had deemed for her.*

FILM

GOOD WILL HUNTING

GOOD WILL HUNTING IS THE STORY OF A REBELLIOUS MATHEMATICAL GENIUS WHO USES HIS INTELLIGENCE TO MASK THE PAIN HE HAS EXPERIENCED IN HIS LIFE. LIVING IN BROOKLYN AND SATISFIED WORKING AS A JANITOR, WILL IS CLEANING AT A UNIVERSITY ONE DAY, WHEN HE NOTICES A PROBLEM SET FOR THE TOP STUDENTS ON A BOARD IN THE CORRIDOR. WILL SOLVES THE PROBLEM IN A MATTER OF MINUTES AND THE UNIVERSITY IS TURNED UPSIDE DOWN TRYING TO FIND WHO COULD POSSIBLY HAVE COMPLETED THE PROBLEM IN SUCH A SHORT TIME.

Eventually the professor who set the problem discovers it was Will who solved it. While the professor is searching for Will, he is arrested for bashing a rival gang member. Sentenced to seek psychiatric help, Will is rescued by the professor and his psychologist, who agree to take on Will's case.

Will's special world becomes the sessions he is forced to attend with the psychiatrist. During the sessions, they challenge each other, progressively letting down their barriers until Will realises it is only through opening up to his past that he will ever be able to explore the potential life has to offer him.

Will's journey into the special world means he has to give up the defence mechanisms he has developed because of years of abuse at the hands of his violent father. Unable to love and commit to anything, Will's journey is in allowing himself to be vulnerable to his girlfriend, Skyler, and his psychologist. In doing so Will learns to release the pain that had been holding him back.

How often in life do we use our past as justification for not moving forward in to the future? Entering the special world almost always means allowing yourself to be vulnerable and at the mercy of the unknown. That is why the first step is so hard.

Watch *Good Will Hunting* and follow Will's journey.

ORDINARY WORLD *Will is trapped in the ordinary world of Brooklyn with his friends.*

CALL TO ADVENTURE *Will meets the psychologist who challenges him to open up about his past and release his anger.*

SPECIAL WORLD *Will's special world takes place in the sessions with the psychologist.*

ENEMIES *Above all, Will's main enemy was his father, but also himself. By allowing his father's actions to dictate his life, Will was refusing his call to adventure.*

ALLIES *Will's main allies are his girlfriend, Skyler, his psychologist and his close friends.*

TESTS *Will's tests come in the form of relationships. Firstly he must learn to trust his psychologist and then he needs to give into the love he feels for Skyler.*

SLAYING THE DRAGON *Will's main dragon is to overcome his fear of commitment and lack of trust of other people. After what he had endured with his father, Will had to learn how to be vulnerable in order to move forward.*

REWARD *Will's reward was finding the will to fall in love and the courage to realise his intellectual potential.*

WILL REALISES IT IS ONLY THROUGH OPENING UP TO HIS PAST, THAT HE WILL EVER BE ABLE TO EXPLORE THE POTENTIAL LIFE HAS TO OFFER HIM.

SUMMARY
THE SPECIAL WORLD

THE SPECIAL WORLD IS A PLACE FROM WHICH YOU CANNOT EASILY RETURN.

THE JOURNEY BEGINS WITH JUST ONE STEP.

THE SPECIAL WORLD CAN BE POSITIVE AND/OR NEGATIVE.

ACCEPT OR REJECT THE JOURNEY.

TO ACCEPT THE JOURNEY YOU MUST TAKE RESPONSIBILITY AND NOT:
- *deny what is happening to you*
- *blame others for your misfortune*
- *justify your progress by ignoring the truth*
- *cling to a victim mentality*

THE SPECIAL WORLD WILL TEST YOUR RELATIONSHIPS WITH OTHERS.

THROUGH THIS TEST A MENTOR WILL REVEAL THEMSELVES.

YOUR DESTINY IS IN YOUR OWN HANDS.

CHAPTER 4
ALLIES & ENEMIES

This is merely a glance of all I mean, for
If he were the sun, I'd be the rays.
If he were the dawn, I'd be the day.
If he were a trail, I'd be the way.
If he were a tide, I'd be the wave.

He is my father, but yet a dream, for if he were the action,
I'd be the means.

HANA ALI

THE MENTOR WHO EMERGED IN CHAPTER 3 WILL HELP YOU CLARIFY YOUR OWN VALUE SYSTEM WHICH WILL BECOME YOUR MOST POWERFUL ALLY ON YOUR JOURNEY. THE REVELATION THAT A PRINCIPLE BASED JOURNEY IS FAR EASIER THAN A COMPETITION BASED ONE LEADS THE HERO TO EXPLORE THE NOTION THAT THE ONLY REAL ENEMIES ARE THOSE INSIDE OURSELVES. WHEN ACTIONS ARE ALIGNED WITH PRINCIPLES, THEY BECOME MORE FLUID AND POWERFUL. TRUE LEADERS EMERGE AND THE HERO SURRENDERS TO THEIR INNER VOICE. IT IS AT THIS STAGE THAT THINGS SEEM TO BECOME CLEARER FOR THE HERO. THE HERO NOW STANDS FOR SOMETHING AND THUS BY LISTENING TO THE INNER VOICE, THE HERO DISCOVERS THAT THE LITTLE VOICE INSIDE WHICH ONCE HELD THEM BACK CAN NOW SET THEM FREE.

A PRINCIPLE-BASED JOURNEY

ONE OF THE REAL DIFFICULTIES WITH MENTORS IS LEARNING HOW TO DISTINGUISH BETWEEN GOOD ONES AND BAD ONES. SOMETIMES CHARISMATIC PEOPLE MAY SOUND FANTASTIC BUT WHEN YOU LOOK BEHIND THEIR MOTIVES, YOU SOON DISCOVER, THERE IS NO REAL SUBSTANCE TO WHAT THEY ARE 'TEACHING' YOU.

At times such as these, it is imperative that you are able to go back to your own value system in order to gain a greater understanding of what is right and wrong. If you are not guided by your principles you will find you are constantly making the same mistakes when making any decision. People who don't know what is important to them tend to waiver when the big decisions have to be made. They are easily led and, above all, they are not true to themselves. Often the really big decisions in life carry huge consequences so, at the time of making them, they may seem an enormous burden. If, however, you remain principle based, there is no real burden, there is only the right decision. Sometimes on the hero's journey you have to stand up for something. When that moment arrives, forget about all the variables and ask yourself, 'What is the right decision?'

Ironically, it is more often than not during your journey that you begin to clarify your own value system and put your principles in place. As a general rule, the stronger your principles, the more likely you are to make the right decisions.

TRUE SUCCESS IN LIFE IS FULFILLING YOUR PURPOSE WITHOUT COMPROMISING YOUR PRINCIPLES.

WHAT ARE PRINCIPLES?

PRINCIPLES ARE GENERALLY ACKNOWLEDGED AS BEING UNIVERSAL TRUTHS WHICH HOLD FIRM IN ALMOST ALL SITUATIONS. AN EXAMPLE OF A PRINCIPLE OF SCIENCE IS 'WHAT GOES UP MUST COME DOWN', ACCORDING TO THE LAWS OF GRAVITY.

Principles in life are a little harder to define. Because human beings change and circumstances differ from moment to moment, it is very difficult to determine exact human principles. During the hero's journey, however, it is essential that you develop a set of principles to assist in making the tough decisions which emerge along the way.

The following story is from a young girl whose life was almost destroyed by her inability to accept the help of mentors.

'I spent my teen years trying to destroy my family. I got so wound up in destruction that I developed a psychosis. At the time I thought my friends were the only people who understood me, but instead of helping me, they introduced me to drugs and alcohol and the spiral started from there. When I look back, I was doing the whole scene just to get attention. I dropped in and out of friendships when people didn't pay attention to me. In fact, I got so caught up in being the centre of attention, I forgot who I was. I started blaming my friends for leaving me, when all along I was the one to blame.

I felt like no one understood what I was going through. I had no principles in my life and my friends had abandoned me. Eventually, I began self-mutilating until I ended up in hospital.

Hospital was the first place I began to understand what principles and mentors are all about. After I had recovered, the nurses took me to see some of the patients who were terminal to show me how I was wasting my life. At first I was really angry at the nurses and hated them for confronting me like this, but eventually I began to catch on.

The nurses at that hospital taught me a few principles that I still live my life by. First, life is too short to waist on self-destruction. Second, don't ever take your health for granted and third, good friends love you for who you are, so always be true to yourself.

Since I left hospital, things have been great in my life. I still make mistakes, but my mentors are there to catch me when I fall. Sadly, of the friends I used to hang with, three have died in the last six months.'

PRESSURE DOESN'T BUILD CHARACTER: IT REVEALS IT.

One great way to learn principles and find mentors is to look at how people have reacted under pressure. The above story shows how circumstances often lead the weak to give up their principles in order to find an easy way out of a difficult situation. The truth of the hero's journey, however, is that if you ignore mentors and compromise your principles in the special world, you can never move on to the reward.

UNDER PRESSURE, PEOPLE REVEAL THEIR TRUE CHARACTER.

HERO
JESUS CHRIST

BEFORE JESUS WAS NAILED TO THE CROSS, PILATE GAVE HIM THE OPTION OF DENYING HE WAS THE SON OF GOD.

All Jesus had to do was say he was not the son of God and he would have been freed. But for Jesus, the pain of denying who he was was far greater than the physical pain of being put on the cross. He refused to deny his principles and chose instead to be true to himself and his 'father'.

HERO
NELSON MANDELA

SOUTH AFRICAN PRESIDENT, NELSON MANDELA, WAS OFFERED THE CHANCE TO WALK FREE FROM JAIL AFTER 27 YEARS IF HE WOULD ACCEPT A PARDON FROM THE GOVERNMENT. HE CHOSE TO REMAIN TRUE TO HIS PRINCIPLES INSTEAD.

'What freedom am I being offered when my very South African citizenship is not respected? Only free men can negotiate. Prisoners cannot enter into contracts… I cannot and will not give any undertaking at a time when I and you, the people are not free. Your freedom and mine cannot be separated.'

Thus Mandela refused the pardon because of his belief in the principle of equal rights for all South Africans.

HERO
ANITA RODDICK

THE CONCEPT OF STANDING FOR SOMETHING ON YOUR JOURNEY WILL DETERMINE YOUR MOTIVATION ALONG THE WAY.

Many people in society are adamant about the things they are against, but very few actually speak and act for something. A great example of someone who stood for something is Body Shop founder, Anita Roddick. In her book, *Business as Unusual*, Anita outlines her philosophies on business and how they fly in the face of traditional standards set by other businesses. Anita's passionate commitment to issues including human rights, animal rights, and corporate good citizenship have seen her develop a multi-million-dollar industry which stands for a whole new way of doing business.

While taking a stand against animal testing, Anita declared, 'Our campaign to ban animal testing in the cosmetics industry came up against deeply ingrained vested interests of the big players in the industry. When in the late 1980s the EEC threatened to bring in legislation that would actually make animal testing compulsory, it threatened the very cornerstone of our business. At the time I said I would close the Body Shop down rather than comply – and I meant it.'

In the following years, Anita would stand up for numerous causes she believed in, even if it cost her company money. This type of principle-based journey has led Anita to understand her journey is far greater than just building a business.

'It is all too easy in business to be distracted by profits, the technology, the cost-effectiveness, the delivery systems. What is important is to never lose touch with what is at the heart and soul – to remember why you were doing it in the first place.'

TRUE HEROES STAND FOR SOMETHING

CHOOSE YOUR MENTORS WISELY

ONCE YOU HAVE A PRINCIPLE-BASED JOURNEY IN PLACE, IT IS IMPORTANT TO CHOOSE YOUR MENTORS WISELY. VERY OFTEN PEOPLE OF VISION ARE PREYED UPON BY THOSE WHO SEE THEIR POTENTIAL BUT THEN, RATHER THAN HELP THEM, TRY TO HINDER THEM.

Even parents often fall into this category. The best way to judge a mentor is to learn to be honest enough with yourself to be able to listen to the voice of your heart and soul. Above all, this is your greatest mentor on the journey of life. If you can learn to tune into the voice it will help guide you to your true north and lead you to the mentors who can really help.

Mentors have to earn your respect. There is nothing more dangerous in life than blindly following someone. History will show that while there have been many great mentors, there have also been many bad ones. Adolf Hitler, for example, was a mentor and a leader to a whole nation. The lesson we should learn from this is that no matter who your mentors are, they should only ever be a secondary guide to your own heart and soul.

THE COURAGE OF YOUR CONVICTIONS

To stand up to the enemies you will meet along the way, it really helps if:

- You understand who you are.

- You understand what your purpose is.

- You understand the principles which apply
  to your journey.

If these three things are in place, you will find a renewed capacity to face your enemies.

Enemies, of course, can come in many shapes and sizes.
Often they are people, sometimes they are emotions such as doubt or anger.

HERO

KIEREN PERKINS

CHAMPION OLYMPIC DISTANCE SWIMMER KIEREN PERKINS' WIN AT THE ATLANTA OLYMPICS IS A GREAT EXAMPLE OF PERSONAL COURAGE.

Written off by the media and his peers, Perkins was suffering from a mystery illness and only just managed to qualify for the final in Atlanta. It is at times like these that true heroes manage to find something extra and stand up under the pressure.

'There are times when you can get a performance out of yourself that you might not ordinarily be able to find. The final in Atlanta was such an occasion for me, a very defining moment in my life. The Olympics being what they are – diaphragm problem or no diaphragm problem – you lift, rise above it. About three hours out from the race I was starting to worry, really sitting there stewing. It got to the point where I got angry with myself. I have rarely been so upset: upset at what was happening: upset that I was allowing it to happen; upset that I was frightened at what I was about to do.

Funnily enough it seemed that as an eighteen-year-old, I was better at dealing with the pressure than I was at twenty-two.

At eighteen, I just got in and did it. Here I was at twenty-two, sitting there and brooding about all the things that could go wrong.

Anyhow, when I got angry late that afternoon I snapped myself out of it. I told myself, "You've done it before, you know what's required, you've just got to forget about the things that have gone wrong." I knew what I had to do: to get out there right from the start and 'attack' the race, the way I had won races before. I had to lay down the challenge, to make it 'my' race. And on that night in Atlanta that's what I went out and did.'

Kieren's mentor, coach John Carew, has been training Perkins since he was nine years old. Initially Kieren did not show above-average ability in the pool, but under the mentoring of John Carew, he kept improving until, at the Australian trials in 1992, he broke the world 400 m, 800 m and 1500 m records. The following comments from John Carew show how important a mentor can be when you are under pressure in your special world.

'He swam a badly judged race in the 400m at the Barcelona Olympics to be beaten into second place by only 0.16 second by the Russian swimmer, Yevgeny Sadovyi. At this stage of the Games, Kieren was the eighth world record holder to be beaten in the pool. The pressure was such that he said to me: "I don't think I'll be able to go home if I don't win the 1500."

I said to him, "I don't think you'll have any problem doing that so don't worry about it. We're going to win it."

Well, he not only won but again broke the world record in a time described by world swimming coaches as "a swim into the twenty-first century".'

With your principles in order, the right mentor giving advice and the right journey, it is often the case that people find they perform with extraordinary courage to face the challenges of their journey.

Your mentor can teach you how to listen to the voice of your spirit to produce a performance in which you feel absolute alignment with all that is happening around you.

LISTEN TO THE VOICE OF YOUR SPIRIT

HERO

PHIL JACKSON

FORMER CHICAGO BULLS HEAD COACH PHIL JACKSON WAS A RENOWNED MENTOR TO SOME OF THE MOST TALENTED AND DIFFICULT ATHLETES IN HISTORY. THIS EXTRACT FROM HIS BOOK SACRED HOOPS, *EXPLAINS HOW A MENTOR CAN HELP YOU LEARN TO LISTEN TO THE VOICE OF YOUR SPIRIT.*

'When I was named head coach of the Chicago Bulls in 1989, my dream was not just to win championships, but to do it in a way which wove together my two greatest passions: basketball and spiritual exploration.

On the surface this may sound like a crazy idea, but intuitively I sensed there was a link between spirit and sport. Besides winning at any cost didn't interest me. From my years as a member of the championship New York Knicks, I'd already learned that winning is ephemeral. Yes, victory is sweet, but it doesn't necessarily make life easier the next season or even the next day. After the cheering crowds disperse and the last bottle of champagne is drained, you have to return to the battlefield and start all over again.

In basketball – as in life – true joy comes from being present in each and every moment, not just when things are going your way…

Even for those who don't consider themselves spiritual in a conventional sense, creating a successful team – whether it's an NBA champion or a record-setting sales force – is essentially a spiritual act.'

TURNING WEAKNESSES INTO STRENGTHS

HERO

HELEN KELLER

THE FOLLOWING EXTRACT IS FROM HELEN KELLER'S BOOK, THE STORY OF MY LIFE, *WHICH EXPLAINS HOW SHE LEARNED TO READ AND WRITE, EVENTUALLY GOING TO UNIVERSITY, IN SPITE OF BEING BORN WITHOUT SIGHT, HEARING OR THE ABILITY TO SPEAK.*

'I felt approaching footsteps. I reached out my hand, as I supposed, to my mother. Someone took it, and I was caught up and held close in the arms of her who had come to reveal all things to me, and, more than all things else, to love me.

The morning after my teacher came she led me into a room and gave me a doll… when I played with it a little while Miss Sullivan slowly spelled into my hand the word 'd-o-l-l.' I was at once interested in this finger play and tried to imitate it. When I finally succeeded in making the letters correctly, I was flushed with childish pleasure and pride…'

If you are on a journey that challenges you, chances are you will begin to see a pattern in the critical point where you are constantly failing. For many people, this point will manifest itself in a weakness that they need to overcome. Sometimes the perceived 'weakness' can be physical, as in Helen Keller's story. Other times it can be an emotional trait, such as anger, which causes a person to give up. Whatever the case, a mentor is often the key to helping you overcome the weakness and turn it into a strength.

THE POWER
OF THE MIND

IN THE MOVIE MIRACLE MAN, *THERE ARE TWO GREAT STORIES ABOUT THE POWER OF THE MIND. THE FIRST RELATES TO AN ELEPHANT AND THE SECOND TO A DEEP FREEZE.*

In the United States, a man found himself trapped in the freezer compartment of a goods train. With no way to get out and no hope of anyone knowing he was in there, the man resigned himself to the fact that he was going to freeze to death. And he did.

However, when the train finally reached its destination and the freezer was opened, it was revealed that the freezer had never, in fact, been turned on. The man had literally willed himself to death.

And what about the elephant? Well, the average circus elephant is trained from a very young age, so that when it is tied to a stake, it cannot escape. This makes good sense until you consider that even when the elephant is fully grown and capable of pulling out a stake ten times as big, it still remains tied to the stake!

It is no coincidence that most people give up in a marathon at about the 30 km mark. It is at about this stage that most runners hit what they call 'the wall'. The wall represents that stage in every journey where you think that you have reached the point where you simply cannot go on any further. For most, this will be the time to quit. But those like Phidippides, the original runner of the marathon, will be able to push through this barrier because they are chasing their dream. Some people experience the wall and say, 'I can't go any further' while others see it as a challenge to greatness.

HERO
STEVE MONEGHETTI

IN LIFE, THE WALL IS OFTEN THE PERSONAL WEAKNESS WHICH STOPS YOU FROM MOVING FORWARD. IN THE FOLLOWING EXTRACT FROM HIS BOOK IN THE LONG RUN, *CHAMPION AUSTRALIAN MARATHON RUNNER, STEVE MONEGHETTI, REVEALS HOW HE MANAGED TO RUN THROUGH THE WALL BY ALIGNING HIS EFFORTS TO A PURPOSE GREATER THAN JUST WINNING OR COMING FIRST.*

'I remember going through the streets and really battling, thinking this is not looking too good. Even though I didn't feel too good early, I thought I'd be right until 30 to 35 km because that's what happened in Tokyo, but I didn't even get that far, it was way before that. Many thoughts were going through my head at that stage. All my hard work had been wasted and in particular the realisation that any medal chance was gone. This is the only goal you've ever had in your life and it's flown out the window. It was very, very tough. The anguish of it all. All you want to do is stop, sit down on the side of the road and cry. But then I thought, I've got to pull myself together, save face. The medal has gone but I'm going to battle on, this is the Olympics, it's for my country.

WHAT STOPS THE DREAM?

HERO

ROCKY BLEIER

WHEN CHASING A DREAM, YOU WILL SOON LEARN HOW COMMITTED YOU ARE TO THAT DREAM WHEN YOU ARE FACED WITH AN OBSTACLE. FOR EXAMPLE, AMERICAN FOOTBALL PLAYER, ROCKY BLEIER, HAD A DREAM TO PLAY PRO FOOTBALL. IN THE SAME YEAR THAT HE WAS DRAFTED TO PLAY FOR THE PITTSBURGH STEELERS, HE WAS ALSO DRAFTED TO SERVE HIS COUNTRY IN VIETNAM. DURING HIS TOUR, BLEIER LOST THE BOTTOM OF HIS RIGHT FOOT IN A GRENADE ATTACK AND HE WAS ALSO SHOT IN THE LEFT THIGH. UPON RETURNING TO AMERICA HE WAS LISTED AS BEING 40 PER CENT DISABLED.

Under these circumstances most people would turn their backs on their dreams and just accept that fate had dealt them a terrible blow, but not Rocky Bleier. His desire to reach his goal of playing pro football was so strong he chose to view his situation as a challenge rather than a crisis. After returning from Vietnam, Bleier remembers what he had to go through at pre-season training camp for the Steelers.

'I have a certain self-discipline, an ability to persuade myself that reality is not what it seems. During that camp, I convinced myself that I actually had a chance to make the ball club. I forced myself to ignore the fact that I still had a noticeable limp.'

Champion yachtsman John Bertrand talks about the 'Tall Poppy Syndrome' stopping his crew from chasing their dream. The Tall Poppy Syndrome is something that causes people to criticise anyone who is trying to achieve success. For example, just go to any football match and listen to the crowd put down the players as they try to chase their dreams. The reason people do this is that they prefer to see people fail because that failure justifies their own decision not to act and chase their dreams.

HERO

CONRAD HILTON

CONRAD HILTON, WHO STARTED THE HILTON CHAIN OF HOTELS, ALSO HAD MANY OBSTACLES TO OVERCOME BEFORE ACHIEVING HIS DREAMS. HE WENT BROKE SEVERAL TIMES AND LOST EVERYTHING HE OWNED IN THE GREAT DEPRESSION. BUT HE TOO HAD MANY REASONS TO STOP CHASING HIS DREAM. IN HIS BOOK, BE MY GUEST, *HILTON TALKS ABOUT THE BEAUTY OF HAVING DREAMS.*

'I myself had looked up from the bottom of the heap with 38 cents in my pocket and seen only a mountain of debt. But even then I had confidence that our way of life offered me the freedom to crawl back up and eventually push out my horizons as far as my vision and strength would carry me... The type of dreaming that appeals to me has nothing to do with a reverie, an idle daydream. It isn't wishful thinking. Nor is it the type of revelation reserved for great ones and rightly called vision. What I speak of is a brand of imaginative thinking backed by enthusiasm, vitality, expectation, to which all [people] may aspire.'

If you have a dream in a certain area it is a very good idea to seek out someone who has already been where you want to go. You would be amazed how many people are out there doing great things and who are willing to help.

You can have many mentors in your life, each doing their little bit, guiding, teaching and often pushing you towards self-discovery. Some are there to catch you as you fall, others to pick you up. Life has a way of guiding these people into your lives, but if you're preoccupied all the time you won't even know they are there.

'I ALWAYS VIEW PROBLEMS AS OPPORTUNITIES IN WORK CLOTHES.'
HENRY KAISER

'LITTLE BEAT BIG, WHEN LITTLE ONE SMART. FIRST WITH THE HEAD AND THEN WITH THE HEART.'

FILM

THE POWER OF ONE

THE POWER OF ONE IS THE STORY OF ONE YOUNG MAN'S JOURNEY THROUGH THE RACIALLY CHARGED WORLD OF SOUTH AFRICA. DURING HIS JOURNEY, PEEKAY IS INFLUENCED BY MENTORS WHO SHOW HIM THE MANY DIFFERENT ASPECTS OF LIFE. DRIVEN BY AN INNER COMPULSION FOR FAIRNESS, PEEKAY'S FIRST MENTORS WERE HIS WHITE MOTHER AND HIS BLACK NANNY. BOTH TAUGHT HIM THE GOOD SIDE OF THEIR RESPECTIVE CULTURES.

Following the death of his mother, Peekay meets two more mentors, one a German piano player and the other a black boxer. The boxer teaches him how to fight and the piano player teaches him how to follow his passion of composing music.

Growing up in both the black and the white worlds, Peekay is eventually forced to choose between the two. His enemies, who include a revenge-driven policeman and his girlfriend's politically-motivated father, set out to bring Peekay down. In a society that is totally geared towards white supremacy, Peekay has to listen to the voices of his mentors and learn to follow his heart, even though he knows this may mean losing everything.

The lesson which emerges above all others for Peekay during his struggle

is that good mentors never force themselves or their beliefs upon you. Instead, they allow you to develop yourself and encourage you to follow your own dream, not theirs.

Watch *The Power of One* and follow Peekay's hero's journey.

ORDINARY WORLD *He is born to white parents farming in an African village.*

CALL TO ADVENTURE *His mother and father die, and he is sent to a Boer boarding school where he is victimised.*

SPECIAL WORLD *His special world is the world of apartheid South Africa.*

ALLIES *The German piano teacher, Doc, the black boxer, Pete, his girlfriend, Maraiha, his English teacher and his nanny.*

ENEMIES *His girlfriend's father, the government and the police guards.*

TESTS *The witchdoctor scene, his boxing match in the black township and standing up to Maraiha's father.*

SLAYING THE DRAGON *As a young boy, he faces the fear of losing his father. As a young man, he faces the fear of accepting responsibility for standing up for his beliefs.*

REWARD *His reward is knowing he can make a difference in the world.*

'I GUESS IT COMES DOWN TO A SIMPLE CHOICE – GET BUSY LIVING OR GET BUSY DYING.'

FILM

THE SHAWSHANK REDEMPTION

WRONGLY ACCUSED OF MURDER, ANDY DUFRESNE IS TAKEN FROM HIS ORDINARY WORLD AND THRUST INTO THE SPECIAL WORLD OF AN AMERICAN MID-SOUTH PRISON. BEATEN, RAPED AND BRUTALISED, ANDY HAS NO-ONE TO TURN TO UNTIL HE MEETS FELLOW INMATE, RED, WHO ADVISES HIM TO 'GET BUSY LIVING OR GET BUSY DYING.

As the relationship develops, both Andy and Red become mentors and allies to each other. In the movie's key scene, despite Red's protests, Andy locks himself in the warden's office and plays classical music through the prison intercom system. 'For that brief moment,' says Red, 'every man in the prison was free.'

As *The Shawshank Redemption* shows us, true mentors will often give up their own personal safety for an ideal. This is why it is often best to judge a mentor on what they do rather than on what they say. Often people can tell you how much they care, but when it comes to actions they seldom follow through. Others say little but are always there when you need them.

Follow Andy's journey through *The Shawshank Redemption*.

ORDINARY WORLD *Andy's ordinary world was working as a banker.*

CALL TO ADVENTURE *Andy's call to adventure came when he was wrongfully imprisoned for murder.*

SPECIAL WORLD *Andy's special world was the prison he ends up in.*

ALLIES *Andy's main ally was his friend, Red.*

ENEMIES *Andy's enemies included the prison guard and a prison gang who brutalised him.*

TESTS *Andy's tests included accepting that life was worth living even though he had been wrongly accused.*

SLAYING THE DRAGON *For Andy, slaying the dragon meant letting go of the past and looking towards the future.*

REWARD *Andy's eventual reward was his freedom and the fact that he helped others achieve a kind of freedom for themselves.*

SUMMARY
ALLIES & ENEMIES

*THE HERO'S JOURNEY
MUST BE PRINCIPLE BASED.*

*PRINCIPLES ARE LEARNED FROM MENTORS
AND THE VOICE OF YOUR SPIRIT.*

*UNDER PRESSURE PEOPLE REVEAL
THEIR TRUE CHARACTER.*

*SOMETIMES A FRIEND WILL REVEAL
THEMSELVES AS AN ENEMY.*

*TRUE LEADERS EMERGE WHEN PEOPLE
HAVE TO DECLARE WHAT THEY STAND FOR.*

*THE JOURNEY ENABLES YOU TO CHOOSE YOUR
FRIENDS MORE WISELY AND TO FACE YOUR
ENEMIES MORE CLEARLY.*

YOUR MENTOR HELPS CLARIFY YOUR
PURPOSE AND YOUR PRINCIPLES.

YOU DISCOVER NEWFOUND COURAGE
WHEN YOUR PURPOSE AND PRINCIPLES
ARE IN ALIGNMENT.

THE JOURNEY EXPOSES YOU AS BEING YOUR
OWN WORST ENEMY AS WELL AS YOUR
GREATEST ALLY.

YOUR MENTOR TEACHES YOU TO LISTEN
TO THE VOICE OF YOUR SOUL AND TO DARE
TO DREAM.

DISCOVER THAT THE VERY THING YOU
THOUGHT WOULD HOLD YOU BACK IS OFTEN
THE THING WHICH WILL SET YOU FREE.

CHAPTER 5
TESTS & CHALLENGES

Never give in. Never, never, never, never!
Never yield in any way great or small,
except to convictions of honour and good sense.
Never yield to a force
and the apparently overwhelming might of the enemy.

WINSTON CHURCHILL BRITISH STATESMAN

DURING MOST CHALLENGES, THERE WILL BE A TIME WHERE THINGS BECOME SO DIFFICULT THAT WE BEGIN TO QUESTION OUR MOTIVES AND ASK WHETHER THE THING WE ARE STRIVING FOR IS REALLY WORTH ALL THE EFFORT. THESE CHALLENGES MAY TAKE THE FORM OF NEGATIVE FEEDBACK FROM PEERS OR FAMILY, THEY MAY BE THE RESULT OF OBSTACLES WE HAVE PLACED IN FRONT OF OURSELVES, OR EVEN PURE PHYSICAL EXHAUSTION. WHATEVER THE CASE, WHEN THE MOMENT ARRIVES, WHEN THINGS SEEM HOPELESS AND ALL APPEARS TO BE LOST, YOU MUST LISTEN TO THE VOICE OF YOUR SPIRIT AND LET IT GUIDE YOU. SOMETIMES, QUITE RIGHTLY, IT WILL TELL YOU TO STOP, BUT OTHER TIMES IT WILL OFFER YOU JUST THE GLIMMER OF HOPE YOU NEED TO GO ON.

'I WAS ALWAYS LOOKING OUTSIDE MYSELF FOR STRENGTH AND CONFIDENCE BUT IT COMES FROM WITHIN. IT IS THERE ALL THE TIME.'
ANNA FREUD PSYCHIATRIST

ANYTHING WORTH ACHIEVING IN THIS LIFE WILL BE HARD BEFORE IT GETS EASY.

How easy would it have been for Debbie Flintoff-King to have accepted second place with 20 m to go in her 400 m hurdles at the 1988 Olympics? Just days before she was due to leave for the games, her sister Noeline died. In her build-up for the race, Flintoff-King was also very ill. And yet with just metres to go in the biggest race of her life, something inside her willed her to go on. The rest is history. Flintoff-King won the gold medal, saying afterwards, 'I am more proud of overcoming the death of my sister, Noeline and my sickness, than the actual race.'

History is full of people who have inspired others by overcoming tests in order to live their dreams. And, more often than not, you will discover that the lengths to which they were willing to go were in direct proportion to how passionate they were about the dream they were pursuing. Too many people wait for the right moment in life only to discover it never comes along. Things will rarely, if ever, be perfect on your hero's journey and above all persistence, courage and principle centred determination will be your best allies.

HERO
THE ABRAHAM LINCOLN JOURNEY

THERE ARE NO SHORTCUTS IN LIFE

Abraham Lincoln 'failed' for 29 years before he eventually achieved his goal. Despite being born into poverty, suffering from two nervous breakdowns and losing eight elections, Lincoln never lost sight of his dream and eventually went on to become one of the greatest leaders of the nineteenth century. Lincoln's journey to the presidency was a long and difficult one with many tests along the way.

1831   Failed in business
1832   Defeated for the legislature
1833   Second failure in business
1836   Suffered nervous breakdown
1838   Defeated for speaker
1840   Defeated for elector
1843   Defeated for congress
1848   Defeated for congress
1855   Defeated for senate
1856   Defeated for vice-president
1858   Defeated for senate
1861   ELECTED PRESIDENT

A significant part of the hero's journey is understanding that defeat and failure are more common than triumph and success. Indeed, most people who have been successful tend to attribute their success more to their failures than to their triumphs. Although we don't all aspire to become president of the United States, we are faced with tests and challenges on a daily basis which may cause great difficulty in the process of our hero's journey.

> **'I FELT SAD TO HAVE DROPPED OUT OF THE SUMMIT ATTEMPT. THE LEG HAD WORKED SO WELL, BUT THEN THE PAIN HAD STARTED. I KNEW THAT TO CLIMB HERE ONLY TEN WEEKS AFTER THE LAST OPERATION WAS INVITING FRESH INJURY, BUT I WAS GLAD I HAD TRIED. AND THERE WAS ALWAYS NEXT YEAR.'**
> **JOE SIMPSON** MOUNTAINEER

NEVER GIVE IN, NEVER!

The concept of never giving in is a difficult one to understand. It is not simply a matter of refusing to give in, under any circumstances. For example, many great mountain climbers have found themselves within sight of conquering Mount Everest and then have chosen to turn back because the weather conditions posed too much of a risk for them to continue.

This is not giving up, it is simply changing direction because, while giving up on your short-term goal, you are not giving up on your dream. The mountain will always be there to climb and one thing is for sure: it's a lot easier to do it when you alive than when you are dead.

Keep in mind that, when striving for the fulfilment of your dreams and your long-term goals, you will sometimes have to give up on some of the paths you might have chosen to get there. Often, that will take more strength than going on. Can you imagine what it must be like to get your team within striking distance of the summit on Mount Everest – and then having to tell them to turn back!

Never giving up is not so much about refusing to quit as it is about understanding that there are more ways than one to reach your goal. As long as in quitting one path, you are choosing to follow another – with the knowledge you gained from your last journey – you are not giving up, you are just changing direction.

Sometimes never giving in means accepting that even the most unfair circumstances should not stop you from trying to follow your hero's journey.

JOHN'S STORY

The story of teenager John Martin is a good example of this.

'I grew up with my fair share of anger. As a black kid adopted by a white family, I was constantly reminded how different I was. Because I was never very good at school, I spent my early teen years learning how to fight in order to get attention. I never really took responsibility for anything and just mucked around and bullied other kids. I enjoyed it but my life wasn't heading anywhere.

One night in Year 7 everything changed for me. I got home from school and noticed Dad's car in the driveway with the engine still running. That was strange because he usually got home well after me. I went over to look at the car and noticed it was full of smoke. Then I noticed the hose running from the back exhaust.

The car was locked and I couldn't see inside, so I smashed the back window. My dad was lying in the back. I pulled him out and tried to give him mouth-to-mouth, but his body had gone all hard and his skin was really grey. I couldn't revive him.

The event was my call to adventure in many ways and it changed my life. Suddenly I went from being an angry kid with no responsibility to being the man of the house and having to emotionally support my family. The test helped me really grow up fast.

I started seeking professional help for my anger management and even started to do a bit of counselling myself. Working with young kids in trouble has become a real calling for me now because I think I understand what they are going through. Hard-edged kids are just the same as everyone else, but sometimes the challenges they have faced are so overwhelming they can't find a way back…That's where I was lucky. For me, the tests and challenges I faced made me wake up to myself, I only wish now I could have done it sooner.'

HERO

THE MAN WHO WOULD NOT BE DEFEATED – A TRUE STORY

IT WAS 19 JULY 1971 AND A YOUNG MAN IN HIS MID-TWENTIES HAD JUST FULFILLED A LIFELONG DREAM BY FLYING AN AEROPLANE SOLO FOR THE FIRST TIME. THAT AFTERNOON, AS HE RODE HIS BRAND NEW HONDA 750 INTO SAN FRANCISCO – KNOWING IT TO BE THE MOST POWERFUL MOTORCYCLE ON THE ROAD AT THAT TIME – A TRUCK CUT ACROSS IN FRONT OF HIM AS HE APPROACHED AN INTERSECTION.

With no time to respond, Mitchell slammed into the side of the truck, crushing his elbow and cracking his pelvis. Simultaneously, the cap of his petrol tank flew off spilling petrol over him and the bike. The poor man became a human bonfire. Fortunately, a salesman on the corner car lot ran out with a fire extinguisher and put the flames out.

Medical statistics say if you receive burns to over 70 percent of your body you usually die. Many people who receive burns to 60–70 percent of their bodies only survive for a short period due to the intense pain and trauma to the body and nervous system.

Mitchell woke up in hospital two weeks later with burns to 65 percent of his body. He lost much of the skin from his face and would have lost his eyesight if he hadn't been wearing contact lenses.

His fingers melted to the palms of his hands and the doctors had to suspend his arms apart, exposing millions of nerve endings. The slightest of drafts sent excruciating pain through his whole body.

Before this point, Mitchell's greatest fear had been the fear of dying but now his greatest wish was to die. A month after the accident he turned to his nurse saying, 'I've died, I am dead. This is all a fantasy. I didn't survive the accident at all. I'm actually dead'. He had to be taken out into the park so he could hear birds singing and children playing before he believed it was all real. In four months he had 16 skin graft operations. As he said later, 'If you started this process one hundred per cent healthy, you'd soon be pushed to the limit. When you start it in agony and three-fourths dead, it is truly no picnic.'

Mitchell went through a phase of self-pity and searched for someone to blame. But he had to acknowledge that he had stared death square in the face and chosen to postpone it. He could have taken the easy way out. Instead, he came to truly value life's opportunities. He made a list of all the things he wanted to achieve, crossed off those which were no longer viable and found he was still left with a list that would fill a thick exercise book.

Against the odds, Mitchell was flying again two months after leaving hospital. Within three years he was a millionaire and had bought his own plane.

Three and a half years after his motorbike accident, Mitchell was flying friends to San Francisco when the hydraulics failed shortly after take-off. The plane did a belly flop back down onto the runway. His three friends walked away without a scratch. Mitchell, on the other hand, had severely damaged his spinal cord and was told by the doctors he would never walk again. The following is an extract from his book *The Man Who Would Not Be Defeated*.

'I was devastated. It was the most incredible of the incredible. I had spent four years recovering from the most devastating injury a human being can incur and lived. It had been the battle of a lifetime, and I had won it. If anyone deserved smooth sailing for the rest of his life, I was the guy. It simply seemed to be too much for one person to bear. I lay in that bed. I wondered if there was anything left of my life. Why me? No one had an answer to that one.

But now I had little time to mope. My support system was far bigger than it had been when I was burned. Literally hundreds of folk from Crested Butte made the five-hour drive to see me. They came

'IN TIMES OF CRISIS ON YOUR JOURNEY, LISTEN QUIETLY AND PATIENTLY TO THE VOICE OF YOUR SPIRIT; IT WILL GUIDE YOU.'

just to tell me they cared, just to encourage me. I came to see, more than ever before, that friends are 'investments' that offer protection in a crisis that no insurance policy can give.'

While he was lying in hospital feeling very sorry for himself, a woman from his home town called him. A year before, Mitchell had offered her advice to help her with her battle with cancer. She reminded him of his words. 'You said something to me that I will never forget. You told me, "It's not what happens to you. It's what you do about it." Do you still believe that Mitchell?'

After being reminded of his own words, Mitchell embraced his life once again, and not long after leaving hospital he became mayor of his town and then ran for the senate. He seriously contemplated running under the slogan, 'Send me to the Senate! I won't be just a pretty face!'

If Mitchell's accident had happened for a reason, it was to enable him to appreciate life so much more. He now had the opportunity to travel and share his experiences; to motivate and empower those he spoke to; to share his story with others and find his own inner peace in the process.

'LIFE IS MADE UP OF SMALL PLEASURES, HAPPINESS IS MADE UP OF THOSE TINY SUCCESSES. THE BIG ONES COME TOO INFREQUENTLY. IF YOU DON'T HAVE ALL OF THOSE ZILLIONS OF TINY SUCCESSES, THE BIG ONES DON'T MEAN ANYTHING.'
NORMAN LEAR

The key to understanding this chapter is to acknowledge that if your journey is worth taking and your destination worth reaching, you will face many, many obstacles along the way. At times those obstacles may appear to be impassable. Obviously, Mitchell can no longer fly a plane but he can still travel. He can still use his experience to inspire others to realise their dreams. And he has his reward – in his mind, he is still flying that plane through the inspiration he gives to other people.

A vital point worth remembering is that as long as your journey is dictated by what happens inside you and not by the environment around you, you can't give up! Whatever your journey is, whatever your purpose is, remember IT IS YOUR JOURNEY. Make it consume your life, think about it every day, align everything you do in life to it until you feel empty without it. When you have made that kind of commitment, when you love doing the thing you do so much you can't even perceive a life without it ... then giving up just isn't an option, you'll do whatever it takes. And the beautiful thing about it is, whatever it takes is up to you. After all, it's your journey!

All human beings have a need to take this journey, that's why so many people challenge themselves. Some bungee-jump, parachute, walk across coals, or jump off the high tower at the pool. Others take up intellectual pursuits, becoming a scientist or an economist or a lawyer, all of which involve dedication and belief in the goal. Others become painters and novelists and poets and musicians and parents – to be a parent might be the most common challenge of all, but it is a tremendously important one. To be a good nurturer and raise the next generation with care and foresight is both a responsibility and an honour.

When we slay our fears, we are conquering those parts of ourselves that say 'I can't'. Every time we confront our fears, every time we challenge our personal maps and struggle to discover the truth, we fight a dragon. And every time we choose to take a risk and stand up for what we believe in, we slay a dragon and walk further down the path toward self-fulfilment.

'TO PUSH ONESELF TO ONE'S LIMITS INEVITABLY INVOLVES RISK, OTHERWISE THEY WOULD NOT BE ONE'S LIMITS. THIS IS NOT TO SAY THAT YOU DELIBERATELY TRY SOMETHING YOU KNOW YOU CAN'T DO, BUT YOU DELIBERATELY TRY SOMETHING WHICH YOU ARE NOT SURE YOU CAN DO.'
WOODROW WILSON SAYRE

HERO
JIM STYNES

'I COULD ONLY LOOK AT ROBERT FLOWER WITH NOTHING LESS THAN TOTAL SHAME AND HUMILIATION. I KNEW VERY WELL THAT FLOWER HAD ONE LAST AMBITION IN FOOTBALL – TO PLAY IN A MELBOURNE PREMIERSHIP SIDE … AND I BELIEVED I HAD ROBBED HIM OF THAT CHANCE … I SHOWERED IN A BLUR OF THOUGHTS. WHY ME? WHAT HAD I DONE TO DESERVE THIS?'

Former AFL player, Jim Stynes has faced many tests in his life. Plucked from obscurity as a teenager in Ireland, Jim was brought to Australia to play football for the Melbourne Football Club. In only his fourteenth senior game, he made a mistake that would cost his club a place in the AFL Grandfinal.

'When I arrived in Melbourne at only 18 years of age, I knew only one other person in the country. After starting in the big time with the Melbourne Under 19s I moved up into the Reserves. Halfway through my second season things turned sour and I was basically sacked and told to go and play with a second division VFA Club, Prahran. For me, that's where the hero's journey could have ended, but for some reason I chose not to quit.

I was so proud of myself the following year when I proved them all wrong and ended up not only making the Melbourne senior team but managing also to be a

part of their first finals campaign for 26 years. We'd won our first two finals games by an average of 100 points. We were on a roll, and Robbie Flower, a champion who had played with the club for 17 years, was about to realise his greatest dream and play in an AFL grand final. Only Hawthorn stood in our way.

For match day, the Melbourne Football Club flew my parents out from Ireland to watch their first ever game, and in front of 84 000 people, we were 22 points up at three quarter time and looking great. We were nearly there. After 26 years Melbourne were going to play in a grand final!

Somehow Hawthorn had eroded our lead down to four points but even with seconds to go we still had it in the bag. Their key forward, Gary Buckenara was awarded a free kick 50 meters out from goal but even Buckenara was going to struggle to make that distance. Then the unthinkable happened. In the heat of the moment, I spotted an opponent, DiPierdomenico, free and closer to goal and rushed across to pick him up. This was the most crucial mistake of my playing career. I had run between Buckenara and the player on the mark, a technical infringement resulting in a 15 metre penalty to Hawthorn. So now

> **'THE LESSONS I LEARNED IN FOOTY WERE REALLY LESSONS IN LIFE. IT'S THE OLD STORY, YOU CAN BURY YOUR HEAD IN THE SAND WHENEVER YOU FAIL A TEST AND PRETEND IT DIDN'T HAPPEN, OR YOU CAN GET UP AND TRY TO DO SOMETHING ABOUT IT. AT THE TIME, IT MAY SEEM THE WORST THING THAT COULD EVER HAVE HAPPENED TO YOU, BUT THE HARDER YOU WORK, THE MORE SENSE THE CHALLENGE YOU FACED SEEMS TO MAKE.'**
> JIM STYNES

Buckenara was shooting from just 40 metres out. Needless to say he put it straight through the middle.

The crowd was stunned. We had lost by two points and we wouldn't be playing in the grand final. In that one moment, my whole life changed. In front of over 80 000 spectators, millions watching on TV, my best mates, my teammates, and my family, I had just made the biggest mistake of my life. From being one of the great success stories of the competition, I was suddenly reduced to being its greatest failure. My whole world had collapsed and there was absolutely nothing I could do about it.

Suddenly, I was forced to ask myself who I was and what I really wanted out of sport. I had only played 12 games in total, so no-one had really taken any notice of this young Irish kid before. After the '87 finals series, however, it seemed everybody knew who I was. People would come up to me in the street and say, 'Hey, aren't you the guy who ran across the mark and cost Melbourne a place in the grand final?'

The more I heard, the more I started to believe I was a failure. My hero's journey had taken a decided turn for the worse.

You see, throughout the whole event the thing that kept coming back to me was that I was a failure because of what other people thought of me. My ego kept chanting to me, "What will other people think of me now?"

I ran away to Europe where no-one knew what Aussie Rules was, let alone what I had done. Until then I had never understood the true meaning of the saying, 'you can run but you can't hide.' As I was leaving Paris on my way back to Ireland, I was standing on a packed bus at 6.30 in the morning and this guy looked at me and said, 'Hey, aren't you that guy who ran across the mark?' I nearly passed out. So for the next three weeks at home in Ireland, I pondered my life and I realised that I might be able to run from others but I could never run from myself. And at the end of the day when you look into the mirror, it is not what other people think of you that matters, it is what you think of yourself. Until you've taken the time to learn who you really are, it's a hard lesson to understand.

In my hero's journey, I was at the crossroads. Was I going to give in or was I going to fight it? Was I going to slay my personal dragon and turn this failure into a success?

So I made a commitment to myself that I was not going to be remembered as the guy who ran across the mark but as the guy who made a mistake, learned a lesson and went on to do great things anyway. I realised that making mistakes gave me a chance to learn something and that failure is, more often than not, the first step to success. I went back out in '88 determined to be the best I could be. Every week I played as though I was playing my last game. This lesson has brought me many rewards including winning a Brownlow Medal, representing Ireland and Australia and holding the league record for consecutive games played.

All of us have had to face fears and tests that have scared the hell out of us. If we accept these experiences as challenges and realise they all happen for a reason then they will help us and allow us to grow and understand ourselves more. The more we understand ourselves, the clearer we become about what we truly want in life.'

The lesson Jim learned from his mistake has helped him to go on and found, along with fellow author Paul Currie, one of the most successful youth training programs in Australia: Reach.

GET USED TO TESTS & CHALLENGES

If we really want to get in touch with our spirit and let it guide us much more in our lives, we have to go beyond the labels given to us and those we place on other people. As you start to search deeper within yourself and begin to question your own beliefs, values and attitudes towards life, you are automatically expanding your world and the people you come into contact with. Living the hero's journey is like an awakened life where you take the blinkers off your eyes, and see the world for the challenges and possibilities it provides.

Developing the self discipline and resilience to endure arduous tests and challenges is a big part of the hero's journey. This does not come easily. Great painters spend years training their skills, athletes endure enormous pain for 60 seconds of an event, and actors deal with knock-back after knock-back before they get the part they are after.

Most people living in the ordinary world, look at the lives of 'successful people' and ask how can they be so amazing. The answer is simple – they are not amazing. They are just ordinary people on extraordinary journeys. Occasionally, a superstar like Ian Thorpe emerges with talent that propels him toward success faster that most, but talent does not overcome laziness, talent does not overcome fear, and talent does not overcome history, people do.

In our society, particularly in Australia, people tend to avoid the hero's journey for a whole host of reasons. What about you? What sort of hero do you want to be? Remember, heroes come in all shapes and sizes. Heroes are great parents, they help others, they contribute to a better society, they complete small anonymous actions. A hero is anyone who is striving to be the best they can be while supporting and loving others in the process. And above all, a hero is someone who triumphs over adversity while remaining true to their principles.

The only time to be afraid of tests and challenges is when you are not honest with yourself. And when you are afraid your dark side will be revealed in the results. As Nelson Mandela points out it is your light not your darkness which should frighten you most.

'OUR DEEPEST FEAR IS NOT THAT WE ARE INADEQUATE.

OUR DEEPEST FEAR IS THAT WE ARE POWERFUL BEYOND MEASURE.

IT IS OUR LIGHT NOT OUR DARKNESS WHICH FRIGHTENS US.

WE ASK OURSELVES: WHO AM I TO BE BRILLIANT GORGEOUS, TALENTED, FABULOUS?

ACTUALLY WHO ARE YOU NOT TO BE?

YOUR PLAYING SMALL DOESN'T SERVE THE WORLD.

THERE IS NOTHING ENLIGHTENED ABOUT SHRINKING SO THAT OTHER PEOPLE WON'T FEEL INSECURE AROUND YOU.

WE WERE BORN TO MANIFEST THE GLORY THAT IS WITHIN US.

IT IS NOT JUST WITHIN SOME OF US; IT IS IN EVERYONE.

AND WHEN WE LET OUR LIGHT SHINE, WE UNCONSCIOUSLY GIVE OTHER PEOPLE PERMISSION TO DO THE SAME.

AS WE ARE LIBERATED FROM OUR FEAR, OUR PRESENCE AUTOMATICALLY LIBERATES OTHERS.'

NELSON MANDELA 1994 INAUGURAL ADDRESS

NEVER GIVE IN TO THE CRITICS

'I KNOW WHAT I'M DOING; I CRITICISE MYSELF TO DEATH. I'M NOT WORRIED ABOUT WHAT OTHER PEOPLE SAY ANYMORE.'

KATE CEBERANO SINGER

Usually, anyone who is truly happy and fulfilled in their own journey will seldom feel the need to criticise others. If you are in a group that puts others down, ask yourself what this says about yourself and your own journey.

WHY DO PEOPLE CRITICISE?

There are two types of critic: those who tell you honestly about your performance and those who criticise you because of their own insecurities. The first type of criticism is valuable and will help you set the standards you need to achieve success. This type of critic might be the mentor we talked of in the last chapter, someone to trust and listen to. But the second type, the one we'll be talking about in this chapter, is trying to cage you in.

The fact is, most people choose to criticise because it is the safest option. To criticise is an easy option because, to do so, you don't actually have to do anything. Critics love it when people stumble because it justifies the fact that they have never had the courage to achieve their dreams, so they gain great satisfaction in seeing others encounter difficulties.

So, in effect, the critics put others down to try and build themselves up. Very rarely do you find a critic actually on a journey themselves; they tend to be spectators.

Make a list of all the critical things that are said at your school and the effects they have on different people.

What do you think could be done to stop a lot of criticism?

NOTHING IN THE WORLD CAN TAKE THE PLACE OF PERSISTENCE.

TALENT WILL NOT; NOTHING IS MORE COMMON THAN UNSUCCESSFUL MEN WITH TALENT. GENIUS WILL NOT; UNREWARDED GENIUS IS ALMOST A PROVERB.

EDUCATION ALONE WILL NOT; THE WORLD IS FULL OF EDUCATED DERELICTS.

PERSISTENCE AND DETERMINATION ALONE ARE OMNIPOTENT.

CALVIN COOLIDGE, THIRTIETH PRESIDENT OF THE UNITED STATES

BEING COMFORTABLE AND BEING COMFORTABLE WITH YOURSELF ARE TWO DIFFERENT THINGS.

WHY DO PEOPLE GIVE UP?

His Holiness, the Dalai Lama, believes the purpose of life is to seek happiness. While this may seem an easy road to follow, when you begin to understand the difference between pleasure and happiness, you begin to see that seeking happiness is a lifetime journey.

The Dalai Lama himself has led a very turbulent life. The son of poor Tibetan farmers, the Dalai Lama's journey saw him rise to prominence to become the undisputed leader of Tibet at the age of fifteen. During this time, Tibet was invaded by the Chinese and in 1958, the Dalai Lama was forced to flee the country and live in exile.

Despite the enormous suffering both he and his people have endured at the hands of the Chinese, the Dalai Lama still manages to preach the doctrine of happiness and forgiveness.

In doing so, however, the Dalai Lama is quick to point out the difference between happiness and pleasure. In short, pleasure is a short-term thing, often a physical sensation which never lasts. Alcohol and drugs, are good examples. In the initial stages, both usually bring instant pleasure, but in the long run, they rarely, if ever, bring happiness.

In this way, drugs and alcohol are often tests to see how hard we are willing to pursue happiness. Happiness often requires lots of hard work. It often requires giving up short-term pleasure for long-term happiness. According to the Dalai Lama, one of the secrets to gaining this type of attitude is to learn **it's not to have what we want that counts but rather to want what we have**. In other words, so long as you rely on outside motivations and forces to help you overcome tests and challenges, you will always struggle.

The real power is inside you already.

'IT'S OK TO FAIL
AS LONG AS YOU LEARN'

HERO
BRIGITTE MUIR

IT TOOK HER FOUR ATTEMPTS AND 39 YEARS TO DO IT BUT ON THE 27 MAY 1997, BRIGITTE MUIR BECAME THE FIRST AUSTRALIAN FEMALE TO REACH THE TOP OF MOUNT EVEREST. HER HERO'S JOURNEY BEGAN IN THE TINY TOWN OF NATIMUK IN THE WIMMERA, AND ENDED AT THE HIGHEST POINT IN THE WORLD.

Along the way she had climbed the highest mountains on seven continents and in 1996, during preparation, she had been involved in a fatal expedition, cut short by a snowstorm which killed eleven other climbers.

According to her husband, Jon Muir, Brigitte's greatest asset is her 'mental and emotional strength.'

'Most men,' he continues, 'have got no idea what true strength is. They think they've got it, muscles and so on. That is a small part of strength.'

In the end it was Brigitte's spirit which took her to the top of Everest. As her husband points out, 'What is worthwhile in life? I think it is worth living and dreaming. If you don't you may be dead anyhow – inside. It may not be easy, life isn't easy, but dreams keep you alive.'

'HATE PUT ME IN HERE AND LOVE IS GONNA BUST ME OUT.'

FILM

HURRICANE

WRONGLY CONVICTED OF MURDER AND SENTENCED TO LIFE IMPRISONMENT, RUBIN 'HURRICANE' CARTER WAS A VICTIM OF PREJUDICE WHO FOUGHT FOR YEARS TO CLEAR HIS NAME. AT THE PEAK OF HIS BOXING CAREER, WHICH COULD HAVE SEEN HIM BECOME WORLD CHAMPION, HURRICANE BECAME EMBROILED IN A MURDER CASE WHICH WAS TO GAIN WORLDWIDE MEDIA ATTENTION.

Dishonest and shoddy police work led to Hurricane's conviction for murder.

Against the odds however, a group of young Canadian students dedicated years of their lives to proving Hurricane's innocence. Eventually, in 1985, his conviction was overturned.

During his time in prison, Hurricane had to overcome many tests and challenges. Firstly he had to cope with the public perception which still, even today, brands him as a criminal despite his conviction being overturned. Rubin also had to learn to accept that he may never leave prison and see his family or friends again. But perhaps the hardest thing for Rubin was to maintain faith desite such a prejudicial and unjust system.

There were many times when Carter nearly gave up, but with amazing strength of character, he managed to pull through and face the biggest test of all; learning to forgive those who put him behind bars. Although this was hard, in the end it proved to Rubin Carter that he could rise above the mentality of those who had put him in prison. He has become an example to millions around the world who have suffered at the hands of prejudicial regimes.

Rubin 'Hurricane' Carter's hero's journey looks like this.

ORDINARY WORLD *Rubin is a boxer aspiring to be champion of the world.*

CALL TO ADVENTURE *Rubin is arrested for a crime he did not commit.*

THE SPECIAL WORLD *USA prisons.*

ALLIES *The Canadian students, his family and the media.*

ENEMIES *The system; the prisons.*

TESTS *Learning to trust others with his future.*

SLAYING THE DRAGON *Learning to forgive those who arrested him.*

REWARD *Rubin was granted his freedom.*

SHE BOUGHT A SMALL TOWN TO ITS FEET AND A HUGE COMPANY TO ITS KNEES.

FILM

ERIN BROCKOVICH

ERIN BROCKOVICH *IS BASED ON A TRUE STORY ABOUT A SINGLE MOTHER WITH THREE CHILDREN. TWICE DIVORCED AND UNEMPLOYED, ERIN IS KNOCKED BACK AT COUNTLESS JOB INTERVIEWS UNTIL, FOLLOWING A CAR ACCIDENT, SHE DEMANDS A JOB FROM HER LAWYER WHO RELUCTANTLY HIRES HER.*

In her capacity as a filing clerk, Erin stumbles across a file that seems to have been suspiciously mishandled. After some initial investigation, she realises a lot of people are dying due to toxic waste from a local manufacturing plant. Against all odds, Erin convinces her boss to take on the case and with her as an assistant, they eventually win.

Throughout the film, Erin is constantly faced with difficulties during her journey. The story is inspirational because it shows how far some people are willing to go in order to live their dreams. During Erin's journey she is tested and challenged many times but it is her positive attitude and willingness to use her perceived strengths that see her through.

ORDINARY WORLD *Erin is an unemployed single mother struggling to raise her children.*

CALL TO ADVENTURE *She has a car crash which leads her to a lawyer who attempts to get her some compensation.*

ALLIES *Her boss, her work colleagues and her neighbour, who becomes her lover.*

ENEMIES *Erin is faced with a system that is designed to keep her down.*

TESTS *She is faced with overcoming the labels and difficulties of being a single mother while trying to maintain a job.*

SLAYING THE DRAGON *Erin must not only demand that others take her seriously, but that she takes herself and her career seriously as well.*

REWARD *Erin wins a large case for her boss's law firm. She is rewarded with a partnership in the firm but most importantly finds she has the self-respect and financial freedom to raise her family on her own terms.*

SUMMARY
TESTS & CHALLENGES

ANYTHING IN THIS LIFE WORTH ACHIEVING WILL BE HARD BEFORE IT GETS EASY.

IF YOUR PURPOSE AND PRINCIPLES ARE ALIGNED, NEVER GIVE UP.

THERE ARE NO SHORT CUTS IN LIFE.

THE DIFFERENCE BETWEEN HAPPINESS AND PLEASURE IS THAT PLEASURE NEVER LASTS AND HAPPINESS NEVER ENDS.

EXPLORE WHY PEOPLE GIVE UP.

DEVELOP TECHNIQUES TO ENDURE THE CRITICS.

LESSONS GIVE US COURAGE.

IT'S OK TO FAIL SO LONG AS YOU LEARN.

MAKE MISTAKES! THEY BECOME AMMUNITION TO FINALLY SLAY YOUR DRAGON.

CHAPTER 6
SLAYING THE DRAGON

But I will forever carry the feeling of victory, and it will serve me in whatever I do. I have seen what is possible and what can happen with the joining of spirit and body. I have seen with amazing clarity the capability of one person performing with focus, efficiency, and fury, with the confidence of someone who has worked as hard as they possibly can. I have looked the dragon in the eyes and I have laid him out flat.

MICHAEL JOHNSON CHAMPION RUNNER

SLAYING THE DRAGON IS THE KEY MOMENT IN THE HERO'S JOURNEY. IT IS THE MOMENT THE HERO FACES THEIR INNERMOST FEAR AND OVERCOMES IT. THE HERO IS OFTEN PROPELLED INTO THIS BATTLE BECAUSE THEY DEVELOP A NEW UNDERSTANDING THAT THE CONSEQUENCE OF NOT SLAYING THE DRAGON IS FAR GREATER THAN THAT OF TRYING TO DO IT AND FAILING. MORE OFTEN THAN NOT SLAYING THE DRAGON HAS TO HAPPEN ALONE. THE HERO MUST SURRENDER TO THE FIGHT AND CALL UPON ALL THAT HAS BEEN LEARNT SO FAR. IT IS THE MOMENT THE HERO IS TESTED AND FORCED TO FACE THE ULTIMATE CHALLENGE. DURING THE FIGHT, THE HERO NEEDS TO SEPARATE FROM THEIR EGO AND DO BATTLE ARMED ONLY WITH THEIR SPIRIT AND SOUL. IN THE END PHYSICAL VICTORY IS NOT IMPORTANT. THE LESSON OF THE BATTLE WILL REVEAL ITSELF. MORE OFTEN THAN NOT AT THE VERY MOMENT VICTORY BECOMES CLEAR, THE TRUE MEANING OF THE HERO'S JOURNEY WILL EMERGE. THE HERO DISCOVERS THE PERSON THEY THOUGHT THEY WERE IS NO MATCH FOR THE ONE THEY REALLY ARE AND THE BATTLE THEY THOUGHT THEY WERE FIGHTING FOR THE ACCEPTANCE OF OTHERS IS SECONDARY TO THE BATTLE THEY WERE REALLY FIGHTING FOR ACCEPTANCE OF THEMSELVES.

> *'BEING YOUR BEST IS NOT SO MUCH ABOUT OVERCOMING THE BARRIERS OTHERS PLACE IN FRONT OF YOU AS IT IS ABOUT OVERCOMING THE BARRIERS WE PLACE IN FRONT OF OURSELVES.'*
> **KIEREN PERKINS** CHAMPION SWIMMER

LEARN TO UNDERSTAND YOUR FEAR

Many people tend to reject fear as being a bad thing, when in actual fact it is a very necessary part of life and of the hero's journey. Once you have learned to accept and then understand your fear, the challenges of the journey become no less daunting, but they do become beatable.

Remember back to the Atlanta Olympics when Kieren Perkins won after being written off by just about everyone in the world (see page 109). Among his first words, as he came out of the pool were, **'If I can win here, I can win anywhere.'**

The statement was not one of arrogance it was simply saying, 'Having overcome my worst fear and all the pressure it placed on me, I am beginning to realise my full potential.'

Take a moment to think back to your childhood and remember the thoughts that used to go through your head. Up to the age of five most of us didn't have any inhibitions and as a result, we believed we could do anything. Sadly, as we get older, more and more people begin to tell us the things we can and can't do, until eventually we start to believe them and develop fears as a result. Some fears are protective (for instance, fear of falling from a high place, or fear of drowning or fear of burning) but a great many fears work *against*, rather than *for*, survival. Some people are so full of fears they are unable to think of anything good about themselves or other people.

The fact is, fear exists only to alert us to danger, not to stop us from reaching our dreams. For those of you who have ever been abseiling, you will always remember that first moment when you stood on the edge of the cliff and tried to overcome your fear of leaning backwards. No matter how hard you tried, no matter how many people went before you or told you it was safe, no matter how many ropes were tied around you, you could not help but be scared. Funnily enough, after a couple of goes most people can't wait to get back up to the top for another turn, to see how far they can jump in one shot! In their haste to have another go at it they rush to the top, they forget to put helmets and gloves on, they hurry the person tying the rope and no matter how many people tell them it's unsafe to jump before they are fully checked, they can't wait to leap off the edge. Why? Because they have overcome their fear. Even though the action they are carrying out is exactly the same, they are no longer scared of it and so it becomes easy!

'TRY A THING YOU HAVEN'T TRIED BEFORE THREE TIMES:

ONCE TO GET OVER THE FEAR, ONCE TO FIND OUT HOW TO DO IT AND A THIRD TIME TO FIND OUT IF YOU LIKE IT OR NOT.'

VIRGIL THOMAS

'I WAS FACING MY TWO BIGGEST FEARS.'

LEARN TO SURRENDER TO FEAR

AMELIA'S STORY

Surrendering to fear sounds like allowing yourself to be defeated. In reality, surrendering to fear and learning to embrace its energy often takes more courage than fighting against it. Take the story of 20-year-old Amelia Laupo.

'It's funny looking back but I can't really remember much about my father. He was an alcoholic and both he and Mum seemed to be working all the time. I never really got to know him as a person. All I can remember was him getting violent all the time. Sometimes mum would even move us out to a hostel.

It was a real shock to us all when my dad finally died and, although I wasn't really sad, I felt a bit cheated by his death. Almost like I wished I could have got to know his good side but he never let me. Fear does that to people. I'm not saying I forgive my father, but I feel sorry for him. He lived his life trapped in fear.

So you can imagine how hard it was for me, when my mum, who had been our protector all our lives, was diagnosed with cancer. I didn't know who to turn to … I just cried alone at night.

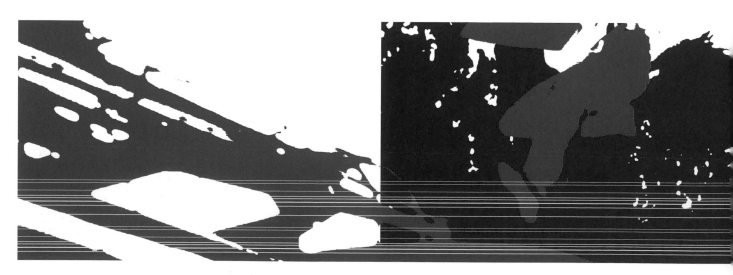

Although I haven't completely slayed my dragons yet, one thing that really helped was admitting to myself and my friends that my mum was sick. I was in this group called Reach Youth working with other youth leaders. At the end of each year we run a concert and it has always been a dream of mine to get up on stage and sing but I was always a bit scared to do it.

I don't know where the idea came from really but, two years ago, I asked if I could sing a song to my mum. Everyone knew she was ill, and on the night I was terrified. I was facing my two biggest fears, singing on stage and accepting my mother's illness.

What's funny looking back now is how beautifully I sung. The audience were blown away and so was I. I can just remember looking at my mum and singing; my heart becoming lighter with each word as though I was singing the cancer out of her body.

I still have a lot to go through and sometimes it's hard to believe in the human spirit, but if you don't what do you have left?'

FAILURE IS PART OF THE JOURNEY

HERO
MICHAEL JOHNSON

WHEN MICHAEL JOHNSON BECAME THE FIRST MAN TO WIN THE 200 M AND THE 400 M AT THE SAME OLYMPICS, MANY PEOPLE DID NOT TAKE THE TIME TO LOOK BACK ON HIS CAREER AND SEE THAT IN ORDER TO DO SO HE HAD TO SLAY MANY PERSONAL DRAGONS.

'... I would not be the runner I am today if it were not for a string of losses dating from my first years in college to my disappointing performance at the 1992 Olympics in Barcelona. It was a harrowing, bitter streak that threatened to define me as someone who couldn't win the big race.
But my reaction was – I think – the force that tempered my strong dedication and led directly to my performance in the 1996 Olympics. I am stronger because of those losses. Without the awful taste of Barcelona in my mouth, who can say how furiously I would have gone after both the 200 m and the 400 m in Atlanta?'

In his book, *Slaying The Dragon*, Johnson talks about overcoming fear as a necessary part of slaying your personal dragons. Johnson's fear was that after failing to win the gold medal at the Barcelona Olympics, he was going to fail again at the Atlanta Olympics. And perhaps in running the 200 m and the 400 m he was attempting too much. In order to cope with this, Johnson chose to meet his fear head on and won both races.

But what would have happened if he had lost both those races?

In *Slaying the Dragon,* Johnson puts it like this:

'Our physical lives are not at all a string of triumphs punctuated by occasional failures, but an elusive chase – a tireless run that eventually will end in failure but that can be marked by frantic and wonderful achievements, a constant battle to take advantage of our time, to accomplish as much as we can before the end.'

In other words, it's OK to fail as long as you use that failure as a lesson to help you achieve success in the future. After all, life isn't about winning or losing, it's about learning along the way.

'IT WAS A HARROWING, BITTER STREAK
THAT THREATENED TO DEFINE ME
AS SOMEONE WHO COULDN'T WIN
THE BIG RACE.'

FALSE FEAR IS TOO HEAVY TO CARRY

To slay your personal dragons on your hero's journey, you need to be able to address your fears and conquer them, remembering that some fears are good but that most are irrational. For example, very few people fear getting into a car and driving to the airport, yet a large percentage of people do fear getting into the plane. When asked why they fear getting into the plane, they say 'because it might crash'. Yet even when you tell them they are 10 000 times more likely to die in the car from a crash than in the plane, they still cannot remove their fear of flying. On the one hand to be up high means having a long way to fall, but on the other to be in a plane means travelling far, fast and safely above the clouds.

In many cases, fear is simply, **F**alse **E**vidence **A**ppearing **R**eal, and the more fears you carry around with you on your journey, the harder it is to overcome the obstacles that stand in your way.

Imagine for a moment that on your hero's journey you are carrying a backpack and that each of the fears you carry around with you is like a one-kilo weight you have to carry in that backpack. Now visualise yourself walking along. The more weights you have to carry, the further over you have to lean to support the weight, and the harder it is to look up and see your goal.

To remove the fear from your hero's journey try the following simple exercise.

1. Assess the situation in front of you and list the positive outcomes of succeeding. Next assess the negative outcomes of failing at the task.

2. If the lure of success is greater than the fear of failure then take the next step.

3. Now list all the ways you can approach the situation to give yourself the best possible chance of success.

4. Once you have done step three you should go forward with confidence and determination, knowing you have done all that is possible to succeed.

Having completed these four steps the fear will still be there but it will become a positive force not a negative one. You will see that on the hero's journey success is always balanced with failure.

Love is balanced with hate; acceptance is balanced with rejection; fear is balanced with courage; pain is balanced with pleasure; anger is balanced with forgiveness; frustration is balanced with understanding; achievement is balanced with disappointment; stress with relief and loneliness with friendship.

If you want one, you must risk experiencing the other. That is life. That is the balance of the hero's journey. That is the dragon that has to be slain.

Am I prepared to love deeply if that exposes me to being rejected deeply?

Am I prepared to fear greatly if that leads to showing great courage?

Am I prepared to forgive deeply if that exposes me to being taken advantage of?

Am I prepared to let go of anger if that means having to listen to people I don't like?

Am I prepared to try my hardest if that means learning at this time my best was not good enough?

Am I prepared to have faith in myself if that means having to acknowledge my own personal greatness?

This last point is an essential step in slaying your person dragons. It is understanding the difference between self-belief and arrogance. To slay the dragon you must have well-founded self-belief built on the back of a thousand failures and years of effort which have taught you how to be true to your principles. There are no short cuts on the hero's journey.

FAITH IS THE DROP OF RAIN THAT KNOWS A RIVER AND DREAMS AN OCEAN.

SLAYING THE FEAR DRAGON

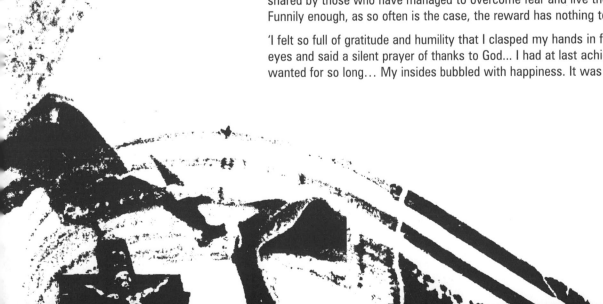

HERO
CATHY FREEMAN

WORLD AND OLYMPIC CHAMPION CATHY FREEMAN USED PRESSURE TO HELP HER WIN AT THE SYDNEY OLYMPICS. IT WAS A WIN THAT UNITED AUSTRALIA AND INSPIRED US ALL TO OVERCOME OUR OWN FEARS AND PRESSURES. WITH ALMOST 10 000 000 AUSTRALIANS WATCHING HER, CATHY CARRIED THE PRESSURE OF EXPECTATION LIKE NO OTHER ATHLETE BEFORE IN OUR COUNTRY'S HISTORY.

But like all hero's journeys, Cathy's dream started years before it became a reality.

'This has been a dream of mine ever since I was a little girl and that's why I got really emotional,' she said after winning the 400 m gold medal. 'Because this has happened to a little girl like me – an indigenous Australian.'

Sitting on the track after her stunning win, Cathy said she felt the strength of her mentors and the support of a nation, 'I was just totally overwhelmed. I could feel the crowd totally over me, all around me, I felt everyone's emotions being absorbed into every pore of my body.'

For Cathy this moment was the culmination of a life's work and her experience is one shared by those who have managed to overcome fear and live the life of their dreams. Funnily enough, as so often is the case, the reward has nothing to do with ego.

'I felt so full of gratitude and humility that I clasped my hands in front of me, closed my eyes and said a silent prayer of thanks to God... I had at last achieved something I'd wanted for so long... My insides bubbled with happiness. It was a dream come true.'

SLAYING THE DRAGON:
A TRUE STORY

AT EIGHTEEN YEARS OLD, KATHI JONES HAD THE WORLD AT HER FEET. HAVING JUST FINISHED SCHOOL, SHE AND HER FRIENDS WERE CELEBRATING AT A PARTY. AT TWO IN THE MORNING THEY MADE A DECISION THAT HAD FATAL CONSEQUENCES.

Following a group of drunken boys out of the party, they rejected a ride home from them and waited for the taxi they had called.

'The boys were so drunk,' recalls Kathi's friend Michelle, 'they could hardly walk to their car. We shouted at them not to drive home but they didn't listen. As if in anger at what we had said, the driver started to do wheel-spins up and down the street. The second time he came past, he lost control. It all happened so quickly. All I can remember is hearing the screeching brakes and seeing the car bounce off the opposite curb and head right for us. I dived out of the way but Kathi was not so lucky. I will never forget the sickening sound as the car crashed into her and pinned her against the brick wall behind where we were standing.'

The male driver of the car lived. His two passengers did not. Since the accident Kathi has been undergoing physiotherapy. Her speech is slurred and her movement is very limited.

'The hardest thing for me,' says Kathi, 'is learning to forgive the driver and get on with my life. What people don't see about road trauma victims is that once all the fuss is over and you are through the hospital, the support is suddenly gone. The bloke who drove the car that night is still alive and walking. I wake up every day and regret where I was standing that night. If I had been the one drink-driving I could live with the fact that I am the way I am now. But it is so hard to forgive, particularly when I know it was just bad luck to be standing where I was. If it weren't for my friends and family, I would not have been able to get through this.'

ALLIES WILL HELP YOU
BUT YOU MUST SLAY YOUR OWN DRAGONS

AS CATHY FREEMAN POINTED OUT AT THE SYDNEY OLYMPICS, HER FRIENDS, FAMILY AND COACHES WERE ALL THERE TO SUPPORT HER, BUT IT WAS CATHY HERSELF WHO ACTUALLY HAD TO RUN THE RACE.

The same will be true for you on your journey. When the moment comes to face your fears, the only person who can overcome them is you. At this point too many people begin to worry about what may happen if they fail. When this happens, try to change the question around and ask yourself, what will happen if I don't try?

If the answer is worse than that which comes from failing, then it is time to face up to it and get moving, time to look inside and realise the person you thought you were is no match for the one you really are.

JUST DO THE BEST YOU CAN
'I'VE KNOWN ATHLETES WHO GET REALLY DEPRESSED WHEN THEY FAIL AND OTHERS WHO GO OFF THE RAILS WHEN THEY HAVE A HUGE SUCCESS.
STEVE MONEGHETTI

Throughout this book we have used the stories of many different people. Some have been successful on the world stage, others in their personal lives. The truth of the hero's journey is that the destination is not the most important thing. While success brings with it public adulation and fame, it should never be the end point of your journey. The end point of the hero's journey should always be happiness, for you and those around you. Happiness is long term. Unlike the short-term fix of winning a gold medal or writing a number one song, happiness will be with you twenty four hours a day, through good times and bad.

The key to success is to make the journey the focus of feelings, not the destination. If at every stage of your hero's journey you can honestly say, I've done my best, then the results take care of themselves.

Following his disappointment at the Atlanta Olympics, champion Australian marathon runner, Steve Moneghetti, talked about coping with failing to reach his goal of winning an Olympic medal.

'I was certainly embarrassed to walk around but the public were terrific. They told me I had done my best and that I had finished and that sort of thing, so it wasn't as negative as I anticipated. I think that's where people undervalue the benefits of living in a country town. The community knows you've put in years of work and they're more disappointed for you. They were actually helping me cope with it.'

'MOST LEADERS TEND TO VIEW TEAMWORK AS A SOCIAL ENGINEERING PROBLEM: TAKE X GROUP, ADD Y MOTIVATIONAL TECHNIQUE AND GET Z RESULT. BUT WORKING WITH THE BULLS I'VE LEARNED THAT THE MOST EFFECTIVE WAY TO FORGE A WINNING TEAM IS TO CALL ON THE PLAYERS' NEED TO CONNECT TO SOMETHING LARGER THAN THEMSELVES. EVEN FOR THOSE WHO DON'T CONSIDER THEMSELVES 'SPIRITUAL' IN A CONVENTIONAL SENSE, CREATING A SUCCESSFUL TEAM – WHETHER IT'S AN NBA CHAMPION OR A RECORD-BREAKING SALES FORCE – IS ESSENTIALLY A SPIRITUAL ACT. IT REQUIRES THE INDIVIDUALS INVOLVED TO SURRENDER TO SELF-INTEREST FOR THE GREATER GOOD SO THAT THE WHOLE ADDS UP TO GREATER THAT THE SUM OF ITS PARTS.'

PHIL JACKSON HEAD COACH OF THE CHICAGO BULLS

SOMETIMES IT TAKES A TEAM TO SLAY A DRAGON

Although the end of your journey will require you to slay your own dragon, very often it is giving in to a team or a relationship that will help you achieve this. Nearly all the great exploits in life, whether they are individual or not, have been successful because they had great teams behind them.

To truly become part of a great team you have to learn to separate from your ego and tap into your spirit.

Those who go on the hero's journey with ego as the motivating force seldom reach a point of happiness. Because ego is so reliant on the opinions of others to keep it inflated, it is only ever a temporary motivation. Spirit, however, is universal. Like Cathy Freeman after her 400 m win in Sydney, spirit connects you to the universal, to something greater than yourself. It is this connection which enables the hero's journey to be fulfilled in the end. It is not the gold medal or the record time or the popularity contest that is the hero's journey, it is the connection to the world and those you share it with.

JOINING THE UNIVERSAL CONSCIOUSNESS

The art of surrender is perhaps the greatest challenge of all on the hero's journey. In this context, surrender does not mean giving up, it means giving in. To give into the force of the hero's journey goes against all the controlling instincts we have been bought up to believe in.

Giving in means learning to surrender to the flow of life, while still controlling your internal compass. By acknowledging that you can only ever control what goes on inside you, you can begin to balance your life and your journey.

No matter what God or life force we believe in, the world is as it is. The hero's journey is learning how to align yourself with 'what is' in such a way that you can express who you are and connect this message to others while allowing them to do the same.

So to slay your dragon, let the world be as it is; let you be as you are; and allow others the right to do the same.

There are many examples of teams and individuals who have reached the moment of synergy when they are totally aligned with who they are and what they are doing. At times like this on the hero's journey, we tend to become greater than the sum of our parts. We tend to excel well beyond our wildest imaginations.

Chicago Bulls coach Phil Jackson says in his book, *Sacred Hoops*, that getting individuals to surrender their self-interest for the greater good of the team 'isn't always an easy task in a society where celebration of ego is the number one national pastime. Nowhere is this more true than in the hothouse atmosphere of professional sports. Yet even in this highly competitive world, I've discovered that when you free players to use all of their resources – mental, physical and spiritual

– an interesting shift in awareness occurs. When players practise what is known as mindfulness – simply paying attention to what is actually happening – not only do they play better and win more, they also become more attuned with each other. And the joy they experience working in harmony is a powerful motivating force that comes from deep within…'

The force that Phil Jackson is talking about is the power of the universe. It is the force which makes waves and opens flowers. It is a force which, if you embrace it, will take you on even more magical journeys than you can imagine.

American 400 m runner Michael Johnson puts it like this:

'Maybe my legacy will be that I was someone who broke world records and won gold medals and ran faster than anyone else up to that point. Those are things I've always wanted. But I also hope that when other people face their own dragons, they can draw on the lessons and examples I've left behind. I feel like an explorer who has charted some incredible region and leaves his map for everyone who wants to go to the same places I have tried to go.

It is clearly not a journey for everyone. People succeed in as many ways as there are people. Some can be completely fulfilled with destinations that are much closer to home and more comfortable. But if you long to keep going, then I hope you are able to follow my lead to the places I have gone. To within a whisper of your own personal perfection. To places that are sweeter because you have worked so hard to arrive there. To places at the very edge of your dreams.'

HOW FAR DO YOU GO WHEN PURSUING YOUR DREAMS?

FILM

SHINE

THERE IS NO DOUBT THAT THE PRESSURE OF PERFORMANCE IS A DRAGON MANY PEOPLE HAVE TO SLAY, PARTICULARLY WHEN THE WEIGHT OF EXPECTATION IS ON THEM. IN THE MOVIE SHINE, FOR EXAMPLE, THE MAIN CHARACTER, DAVID HELFGOTT, HAS TO ENDURE INCREDIBLE PRESSURE FROM HIS FATHER BEFORE HE CAN 'BREAK FREE' AND PERFORM.

Overbearing and violent, David's father refuses to let go of his influence on his son and eventually forces him to choose between his family and his music career. The decision is one that wracks David with guilt.

When David finally does break free and makes it to London, he discovers his mentor, a college professor who takes him on to slaying the dragon by playing Rachmaninoff's *Piano Concerto Number 3*.

Considered one of the most difficult pieces of piano music to play, David becomes totally engrossed in the process of playing. On the night of his final performance, consumed with guilt and torment, David plays the piece perfectly but expends so much energy, he collapses at the end in a nervous breakdown.

After the collapse, David is never the same again. Although he is still a genius

pianist, he is unable to relate to people in a normal way.

The end of the movie leaves us asking an interesting question: how far do you go when pursuing your dreams? The answer to this is not simple. Although David managed to slay the musical dragon he faced, it was his failure to confront the issues he had with his father which led to his breakdown.

Trace David's hero's journey while watching *Shine*.

ORDINARY WORLD *Growing up in Australia.*

CALL TO ADVENTURE *David is accepted to music college in England.*

SPECIAL WORLD *Music college in England.*

TESTS & CHALLENGES *David has to defy his father to leave and then attempts to play the Rach 3.*

ALLIES *His friends and his music teachers.*

ENEMIES *His father.*

SLAYING THE DRAGON *David successfully plays the Rach 3.*

REWARD *David achieves musical fame but fails to win the respect and forgiveness of his father.*

SUMMARY
SLAYING THE DRAGON

LEARN TO UNDERSTAND YOUR FEAR.

SURRENDER AND EMBRACE FEAR AS PART OF THE JOURNEY.

FALSE FEAR IS TOO HEAVY TO CARRY.

PRESSURE REVEALS THE TRUTH.

ALLIES WILL HELP BUT ONLY YOU CAN SLAY YOUR OWN DRAGON.

JUST DO THE BEST YOU CAN.

SOMETIMES IT TAKES A TEAM.

SEPARATE FROM EGO.

JOIN THE UNIVERSAL CONSCIOUSNESS.

CHAPTER 7
THE REWARD

Do not take anything as being forever,
because forever is only as long as today.
Know that the people who are richest
are not those who have the most,
but those who need the least.
That we are at our strongest when life is at its worst
and at our weakest when life no longer offers a challenge.
That it is wiser not to expect, but to hope,
for in expecting you ask for disappointment
whereas in hoping, you invite surprise;
That unhappiness doesn't come from not having something you want,
but from the lack of something inside that you need.
That there are things to hold and things to let go,
and letting go doesn't mean you lose,
but that you acquire that which has been waiting around the corner.
Most of all…
remember to use your dream as a way of knowing yourself better,
and as an inspiration to reach for your star.

NANCY SIMS

HAVING SLAIN THE DRAGON, THE FINAL EMERGENCE FROM THE CAVE LEAVES THE HERO WITH AN INNER STRENGTH WHICH WILL NEVER LEAVE THEM. THERE MAY BE OTHER JOURNEYS TO TRAVEL, OTHER FIGHTS TO FIGHT, BUT THE HERO NOW LIVES WITH THE KNOWLEDGE THAT THEY CAN ENDURE. IN THE END, NO MATTER WHAT THE BATTLE, THE REWARD IS ALMOST ALWAYS THE SAME:

THE HERO LEARNS TO SURRENDER TO LIFE AND LOVE THEMSELVES FOR WHO THEY ARE AND NOT FOR WHAT OTHER PEOPLE WANT THEM TO BE.

THE HERO EMERGES WISER. THEY HAVE GAINED KNOWLEDGE THROUGH EXPERIENCE AND WITH THEIR NEWFOUND INNER PEACE, THEY ARE FILLED WITH THE NEED TO GIVE SOMETHING BACK.

AT LAST SEPARATED FROM THE EGO, THE HERO CAN RETURN TO THE PLACE THEY STARTED AND SEE IT FOR WHAT IT REALLY IS. FOR MANY, THIS MAY BE A BLESSING WHILE FOR OTHERS IT MAY BE THE MOTIVATION TO START A NEW JOURNEY.

WHATEVER THE CASE, THE REWARD EMERGES THE SAME FOR WHOEVER TAKES THE HERO'S JOURNEY: IT IS NOT THE DESTINATION THAT IS IMPORTANT, IT IS THE PERSON YOU BECOME IN THE PROCESS. MAP THE PROCESS, FOLLOW THE DREAM AND KNOW THAT YOU ARE NOT ALONE.

THE REWARD IS OFTEN
NOT WHAT YOU EXPECTED

MIKA'S STORY

INTERESTINGLY, THE END POINT FOR YOUR HERO'S JOURNEY IS OFTEN VERY DIFFERENT TO WHAT YOU EXPECTED. MORE OFTEN THAN NOT, THE END POINT IS THE START OF ANOTHER JOURNEY.

For 21-year-old Mika the reward of her hero's journey was learning to release her emotions by acting on stage.

'All my life I had been overshadowed by a Japanese cultural background which encouraged us to be very inward in our dealing with issues. When my family moved to Australia, I found it very difficult. I was crying all the time, I was carrying so much inside and had no way of letting it all out.

When I look back now all I really wanted to do was to be accepted. That's kind of why I joined a drama group in the first place: to be part of something. I really threw myself into the groups and depended on them for acceptance, but the more I went on that journey, the more I started to alienate my friends and push them away.

In this way I started to hate drama, as though it was my acting and not me that was pushing people away. So instead of acting I started being really honest with people and telling them what I thought about them. That's when I started to get really depressed.

It wasn't until one night I just went on stage and gave a performance from my heart that I realised how much bitterness and anger I had to get rid of. It all came out on stage. It helped me to work through things. I wasn't acting for the audience any more, I was acting for myself.

That's been my reward: to learn the lessons of life and to grow as a result. Whereas I used to go round in circles, I now go in spirals, trying not to make the same mistakes and trying to improve and get a little higher each time.

Funnily enough, my hero's journey has taken me back to teaching acting now; to teach the human spirit and to pass on what I have learned to others.'

There is no real end to the hero's journey. It travels with you forever. In fact, the more you learn the less you know. Wisdom is more about surrender than it is about understanding. Your purpose is often changing and just as you reach the top of one mountain another emerges in the distance.

In his book, *Long Walk To Freedom*, Nelson Mandela talks about the journey of his life never ending. Even after 27 years in jail and a life time full of experiences, Mandela never stopped learning and remained humble about his wisdom. In many ways, the purpose of his life was to free his people, perhaps even the people of the world. Interestingly, his reward came not from the remarkable results of his life but from the knowledge that to be truly free is to be able to live in such a way that enables others to be the same as well.

'Freedom is indivisible; the chains on anyone of my people were chains on all of them, the chains on all of my people were chains on me.'

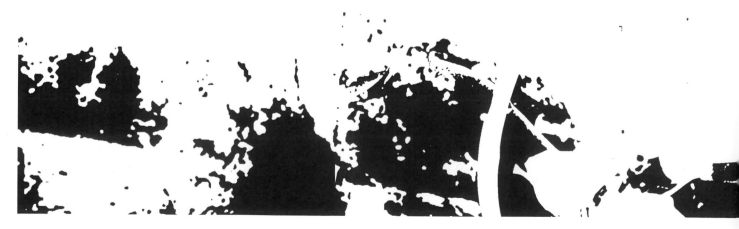

EXPERIENCE EQUALS WISDOM

It was during those long and lonely years that the hunger for freedom of my own people became a hunger for the freedom of all people, white and black. I knew as well as I knew anything that the oppressor must be liberated just as surely as the oppressed. A man who takes away another man's freedom is a prisoner of hatred, he is locked behind the bars of prejudice and narrow-mindedness. I am not truly free if I am taking away someone else's freedom, just as surely as I am not free when my freedom is taken from me. The oppressed and the oppressor are robbed of their humanity.

When I walked from prison, that was my mission, to liberate the oppressed and the oppressor both. Some say that has now been achieved. But I know that is not the case. The truth is that we are not yet free; we have merely achieved the freedom to be free, the right not to be oppressed. We have not taken the final step of our journey, but the first step on a longer even more difficult road. For to be free is not merely to cast off one's chains, but to live in a way that respects and enhances the freedom of others. The true test of our devotion to freedom is just beginning.

I have walked that long road to freedom. I have tried not to falter; I have made missteps along the way. But I have discovered the secret that after climbing the great hill, one only finds that there are many more hills to climb. I have taken a moment here to rest, to steal a view from glorious vista that surrounds me, to look back on the distance I have come. But I can rest only for a moment, for with freedom come responsibilities, and I dare not linger, for my long walk is not yet ended.'

THE GIFT OF THE JOURNEY IS INNER PEACE

HERO

PAT RAFTER

AUSTRALIAN OF THE YEAR 2001, PAT RAFTER IS NOT ONLY A GREAT TENNIS PLAYER BUT A CHAMPION PERSON AS WELL.

Although his sporting journey has taken him all over the world to win many tournaments, including back-to-back US Open titles, Pat has managed to remain humble and modest to the point where his post-tennis career will now focus on his family and helping others.

Pat's 'Cherish the Children' fund was set up by him and his brother in order to use some of Pat's influence to help the young children of Australia. So while Pat will no doubt be remembered for his skill on the tennis court, he will also be remembered for the person he has aspired to be off it.

Perhaps the best example of this is the way Pat has managed to accept his injuries and defeats and turn apparently overwhelming disappointments into personal victories. It is often said that you should judge the calibre of a person by the manner in which they deal with adversity, and, in this arena, Pat Rafter stands alone. Despite the cutthroat world of international tennis, Pat has appeared balanced and so full of inner peace that he has managed to hold his dignity and win as many admirers in defeat as he has in victory.

ACCEPT YOURSELF FOR WHO YOU ARE

One of the great rewards of the hero's journey is the capacity to accept yourself for who you are. Once you have been able to do this you will experience an enormous loss of conflict in your life. Those bouts of self-sabotage will disappear. Those moments of doubt when faced with important decisions will be become less frequent and life will start to reward you with the riches of living in balance. Of course, bad luck and misfortune will still come your way from time to time, but for balanced people, these moments are seen more as challenges than disasters.

The trick with this phase of the hero's journey is to accept that while the fundamentals of who you are will remain the same, the ways in which you express this will always change. Who you are is dynamic and it goes through phases such as those below.

0–5	The selfish learning years
5–10	The relating years
10–20	The growing years
20–30	The exploring years
30–40	The settling years
40–50	Helping someone else on their journey

For many, these phases differ but some heroes discover their reward is actually to end up mentoring someone else on their journey. If you recall back to Chapter 4 on mentors you will remember that you should be very careful when selecting mentors. Perhaps now you will see why. Many mentors try to take on the role too early without having slain their own dragons. This is never a good sign, as often they place too much pressure on you during your journey because inwardly they are subconsciously setting you up to fail at the same place they did. That's why mentors need to earn their stripes.

You can sense the people who know who they are. They project the reward of inner strength.

SEPARATE FROM YOUR EGO

Once you have established who you are and you are confident in that person, the need for ego becomes less and less frequent. You gain so much satisfaction from personal success and balance that you don't need to brag about it to others. You no longer need the reassurance of those around you because you have found the gift of self-love.

Self-love is an often misunderstood concept. It is not arrogance or ego, it is genuine self-appreciation. It is an understanding of the struggle you have endured on your journey and an acceptance of the humility that pervades those who have known great struggle and triumph.

Jon Carnegie often tells the story of his first meeting with world leader, Nelson Mandela. At a reconciliation luncheon inspired by Jon and his students, Jon met with Mr Mandela prior to attending the luncheon.

'I remember asking him what his message would be to those at the luncheon, a guest list which included two former prime ministers, the premier and many other dignitaries. Mr Mandela simply smiled and said in the most gentle voice imaginable, **"My message will be that your greatness is in your smallness."**

I was unsure what he meant by this, but later at the luncheon I found out. Prior to Mr Mandela entering the room, while a young Aboriginal dance troop performed a welcome ceremony, I watched as the many dignitaries fussed over who would sit where and who would meet Mr Mandela first. They lined themselves up at the front table, and waited for Mr Mandela to arrive. When he finally did come in, instead of walking over to them, Nelson made a beeline for the youngest of the Aboriginal dancers, picked him up and embraced him. Of course the cameras went wild and the picture was all over the front pages of newspapers around the country.

At that moment I understood what Mr Mandela had meant… your greatness is in your smallness. It is in your capacity to separate from your ego at all times and see the things that are really important. In his speech later that night, Mr Mandela finished by giving another young boy a scroll of paper which read, 'Judge a nation by the way it treats its children.'

GIVE
SOMETHING
BACK

MOTHER TERESA

Mother Teresa lived what for many may have seemed a self-imposed life of misery. But for someone who has seen the extremes of life as she has, her life of service must have been incredibly rewarding.

So powerful was Mother Theresa's calling to help others, that instead of considering living in the squalor and misery of Calcutta as a difficulty, she embraced it. Although it was not always a pleasurable experience, she actually gained great happiness from dedicating her life to the service of others.

Mother Teresa had connected to something greater than herself. She believed she was doing God's work and given the enormous faith she possessed, nothing could dissuade her from her call to adventure to help the poor. Like Nelson Mandela, Mother Teresa is typical of a person who has understood that contribution is the greatest reward of the hero's journey.

Giving back is one of the most rewarding things you can do. Even simple things like taking the time to write a letter of gratitude to someone who made a difference in your life can be a really fulfilling experience; especially for the person receiving the letter.

'THE MOST DIFFICULT PART OF ANY ENDEAVOUR IS TAKING THE FIRST STEP, MAKING THE FIRST DECISION.'

AS ONE JOURNEY ENDS, ANOTHER BEGINS

Another great reward on the hero's journey is the knowledge that once you have overcome the difficulties of a great journey, you are more ready to embrace the next. Indeed the more you test yourself and attempt different journeys, the more you discover that life is all about little journeys.

HERO
ROBYN DAVIDSON

IN HER BOOK, TRACKS, *ROBYN DAVIDSON RECOUNTS HER YEAR-LONG ODYSSEY CROSSING THE AUSTRALIAN DESERT ALONE, WITH ONLY A HERD OF CAMELS FOR SUPPORT.*

'As I look back on the trip now, as I try to sort out the fact from the fiction, try to remember how I felt at that particular time, or during that particular incident, try to relive those memories that have been buried so deep and distorted so ruthlessly, there is one fact that emerges from the quagmire. The trip was easy. It was no more dangerous than crossing the street, or driving to the beach, or eating peanuts. The two important things that I did learn were that you are as powerful and strong as you allow yourself to be, and that the most difficult part of any endeavour is taking the first step, making the first decision. And I knew even then that I would forget them time and time again and would have to go back and repeat those words that had become meaningless, to try and remember. I knew even then that instead of remembering the truth of it, I would lapse into useless nostalgia. Camel trips, as I suspected all along, and as I was about to confirm, do not begin or end, they merely change form.'

ARRIVE BACK WHERE YOU STARTED AND SEE
THAT PLACE FOR THE FIRST TIME

The very final stage of the hero's journey is the arrival back home. Watch any of the movies we have mentioned and notice how, more often than not, the end point seems to be exactly where the movie began. The trees are the same, the houses are the same, the people are the same. The only thing that has changed is the hero. That's what makes heroes stand out. That is part of the beauty of the journey. Talk to anyone who has travelled overseas through the Third World and retuned to Australia, and listen to how the journey helped them to appreciate what they have right now.

Imagine for a minute losing any one or all of the brilliant things your life has to offer right now and then imagine yourself at 80, having never lost them, but never having taken advantage of them either.

Just by reading this book, you have taken a mini hero's journey. With what you understand now, if you were to re-read the book, you would read it with a very different attitude. You would skip some bits you have mastered, re-read bits that tripped you up, but above all, with each new reading you would find something new; a new journey as rewarding, as challenging, as harsh and as beautiful as the one you are on now.

MY HOPES, MY DREAMS, MY FUTURE

The word 'hero' originates from the Greek language and means 'to protect and serve'. The heroes of Greek myth were people who sacrificed themselves for the greater good. But the heroes of today have taken on a different aspect.

Think now of all the quiet heroes who patch things up and make them work and who face danger and fear with patience and courage. A hero is able to make sacrifices for the greater good. This person may never make it to the front page of the paper, but they will make it into the hearts and minds of others. How? By getting in touch with their own spirit.

Everyone is a potential hero, and that's why we call *your* journey the hero's journey. A hero brings peace, courage, patience and intelligence to the problems that beset every life. She or he may not be able to provide all these qualities at once – he or she might be better in some areas than others – but a hero will do their best with what they have.

Live life to the full and learn everything you can. Forget about being perfect and just try instead to be yourself.

IF I HAD MY LIFE OVER AGAIN, I'D DARE TO MAKE MORE MISTAKES NEXT TIME. I WOULD LIMBER UP. I WOULD TAKE FEWER THINGS SERIOUSLY. I WOULD TAKE MORE CHANCES. I WOULD CLIMB MORE MOUNTAINS AND SKIP MORE RIVERS. I WOULD EAT MORE ICE-CREAM AND LESS BEANS. I WOULD PERHAPS HAVE MORE TROUBLES, BUT I WOULD HAVE FEWER IMAGINARY ONES. YOU SEE, I AM ONE OF THOSE PEOPLE WHO LIVES SERIOUSLY, HOUR AFTER HOUR, DAY AFTER DAY. OH, I'VE HAD MY MOMENTS, BUT IF I HAD TO DO IT OVER AGAIN, I'D HAVE MORE

OF THEM. IN FACT I'D TRY TO HAVE NOTHING ELSE, JUST MOMENTS, ONE AFTER THE OTHER INSTEAD OF LIVING SO MANY YEARS AHEAD OF EACH DAY. I'VE BEEN ONE OF THOSE PEOPLE WHO NEVER GOES ANYWHERE WITHOUT A THERMO-METER, A HOT WATER BOTTLE, A RAINCOAT AND A PARACHUTE. IF I HAD TO DO IT OVER AGAIN, I'D TRAVEL LIGHTER THAN I HAVE. I WOULD START BAREFOOT EARLIER IN THE SPRING AND STAY THAT WAY LATER IN THE FALL. I WOULD GO TO MORE DANCES. I WOULD RIDE MORE MERRY-GO-ROUNDS. I WOULD PICK MORE DAISIES.

DICK LEIDER THE AUTHOR OF THE POWER OF PURPOSE

'LIFE IS LIKE A BOX OF CHOCOLATES. YOU NEVER KNOW WHICH ONE YOU'RE GONNA GET.'

FILM

FORREST GUMP

BORN SIMPLE AND CRIPPLED IN THE AMERICAN SOUTH, FORREST GUMP'S JOURNEY TAKES US THROUGH THREE TURBULENT DECADES OF AMERICAN HISTORY. BY FOLLOWING HIS HEART, FORREST'S HERO'S JOURNEY SEES HIM BECOME A COLLEGE FOOTBALL STAR, A VIETNAM WAR HERO, A WORLD CHAMPION TABLE TENNIS PLAYER AND A MULTIMILLIONAIRE FISHERMAN.

But through it all, Forrest's greatest desire is to win the heart of his lifelong love, Jenny. Throughout the film, Jenny is Forrest's soul mate, but it is only at the end, after all the triumphs and tribulations that Forrest finally manages to win Jenny over by remaining true to himself.

His reward comes in the shape of a baby son who is everything Forrest dreamed of being himself. Simplistic as it is, the theme of the movie is to be found in the line, 'Life is like a box of chocolates. You never know what you're gonna get.'

The reward of the hero's journey is the knowledge that life can throw anything at you. Extreme good and extreme bad can happen to all of us and we have no real control over which is to come next. The only thing we do control is our response to challenges and the knowledge that the heart knows the secrets our mind never can.

Forrest Gump's hero's journey takes this shape.

ORDINARY WORLD *Small town, Southern USA.*

CALL TO ADVENTURE *Forrest is selected to play college football.*

TESTS *Forrest's love for Jenny is tested by the fact she will not return his love as he would like.*

ALLIES *His mother, his friend Bubba and his childhood sweetheart, Jenny.*

ENEMIES *Jenny's alcoholic father, the children who picked on Forrest at school and a society that would not embrace him.*

SLAYING THE DRAGON *For Forrest to win over Jenny, he has to remain loyal to her until she becomes ill.*

REWARD *Forrest's rewards come in the form of his son and the fact that Jenny eventually returns his love*

'I'M YOUNG, I'M HANDSOME, I'M FAST AND CAN'T POSSIBLY BE BEAT.'

FILM

WHEN WE WERE KINGS

WHEN WE WERE KINGS IS A DOCUMENTARY FILM BASED ON THE LIFE OF WORLD HEAVY-WEIGHT BOXING CHAMPION, MUHAMMAD ALI. REVOLVING AROUND HIS 1974 TITLE FIGHT WITH GEORGE FOREMAN, THE FILM EXPLORES ALI'S JOURNEY TO THE AFRICAN NATION OF ZAIRE TO FACE THE UNBEATABLE FOREMAN. THE DRAGON ALI HAD TO SLAY WAS THE FACT THAT DESPITE HIS APPARENT SELF-CONFIDENCE, BY THE NINTH ROUND HE WAS GETTING BEATEN AND THERE SEEMED NO WAY HE COULD WIN. COMMENTATOR, NORMAN MAILER SAYS, 'IT WAS THE ONLY TIME I EVER SAW FEAR IN ALI'S EYES.'

For all those who have ever dared to achieve great things, the moment of fear is the one which defines success and failure. This is the moment when everything inside you tells you, you can't go on – but you do. To go on when faced with this fear takes enormous courage. The dragon Ali had to overcome on that day was not that of winning the fight, but that of being prepared to lose it.

It was this courage that enabled Ali to go on and win the fight and then continue to achieve even greater rewards in life. *When We Were Kings* sees Ali proclaiming his famous catch line, 'I am the Greatest.'

But years later, despite his enormous fame as a boxer, Ali made an even bigger statement to the world when, with his body ravaged by Parkinson's syndrome, he lit the flame at the Atlanta Olympics.

When speaking about his disease Ali says, 'He (God) gave me Parkinson's syndrome to show me I am not "The Greatest", he is. To show me I have human frailties like everybody else does. That's all I am; a man.'

In this way *When We Were Kings* is a metaphor for Ali's life; always challenged, always controversial, always willing to back himself, and always capable of humility beneath the surface of his apparent invincible self-confidence.

Trace Muhammad Ali's hero's journey through *When We Were Kings*.

ORDINARY WORLD The USA before the fight.

CALL TO ADVENTURE Promoter Don King asks Ali to fight Foreman in Zaire.

SPECIAL WORLD The African country of Zaire.

ALLIES The people of Zaire and the Ali camp.

ENEMIES The Foreman camp.

TESTS The postponement of the fight and Foreman himself.

SLAYING THE DRAGON Facing Foreman in the ring after being unable to find his weakness in the first nine rounds.

REWARDS Heavyweight championship of the world and the knowledge that, with faith, he could achieve anything.

SUMMARY
THE REWARD

THE REWARD IS OFTEN NOT WHAT YOU EXPECTED.

KNOWLEDGE THROUGH EXPERIENCE = WISDOM.

THE GIFT OF THE JOURNEY IS INNER PEACE AND STRENGTH.

THE END POINT OF THE JOURNEY IS ACCEPTING YOURSELF FOR WHO YOU ARE.

THE SEPARATION OF SPIRIT FROM EGO IS THE REVELATION THAT BRINGS PEACE.

HAVING SLAIN YOUR DRAGON YOU WILL FEEL THE NEED TO GIVE SOMETHING BACK.

YOU WILL CHANGE AND THIS WILL ENABLE YOU TO SEE YOUR ORDINARY WORLD DIFFERENTLY.

ONCE ONE JOURNEY ENDS, ANOTHER BEGINS.

TAKE TIME TO RECAP WHAT YOU HAVE LEARNED AND START AGAIN.

Kylie

IAN

MARTIN

Dani

Brigitte

Bryce

Bubby

Cathy

Lleyton

Kieren

Karrie

Julia

Louise

Shelley

Jim

Michael

Diana

Ella

ANITA

MATT

Christina

D.L.

PAT

Robyn

JESSE

RUSSELL

Nelson

Forrest

Mitchell

Muhammad

Mother Teresa

NOAH

FURTHER READING

LIONHEART Jesse Martin, Allen & Unwin 2000
Jesse Martin's extraordinary solo voyage around the globe on his boat Lionheart.

DREAM ON Jesse Martin & Jon Carnegie, Hardie Grant 2002
This is an in-depth look at the process of making dreams come true, offering many excellent insights.

MAYBE TOMORROW Boori Pryor, Penguin
The life story of an Aboriginal performer.

THE ART OF HAPPINESS His Holiness the Dalai Lama & Howard C Cuttler, Hodder 1998
A guide to seeking inner peace through the Buddhist philosophy.

LONG WALK TO FREEDOM Nelson Mandela, Abacus 1994
Nelson Mandela's extraordinary fight for his own freedom and that of his people.

THE WINNER WITHIN Pat Riley, Berkley Books, USA 1996
Basketball coach Pat Riley's efforts to build better teams.

BUSINESS AS UNUSUAL Anita Roddick, Harper Collins 2002
How one woman refused to bow to the pressures of business and managed to create her dream.

THE RIGHT MOUNTAIN Jim Hayhurst
An ordinary man's attempts to climb Mount Everest and the lessons he learned along the way.

CATHY FREEMAN Adrian McGregor
Australian legend Cathy Freeman's struggle to rise to the top in both life and athletics.

TRACKS Robyn Davidson
One woman's journey into the Australian desert, alone.

THE EDGE Howard Ferguson
A book for sporting enthusiasts, with quotes and stories from world-class athletes about reaching your full potential.

THE MAN WHO WOULD NOT BE DEFEATED W Mitchell, Brolga 1995
One man's struggle to overcome two incredible life-threatening accidents which left him paraplegic and scarred for life.

AWARENESS Anthony De Mello
A simple, yet profound look at life: a series of simple short stories and metaphors with a deeper message.

THE GREATEST MIRACLE IN THE WORLD Og Mandino
All of Og Mandino's books are quick and easy to read, with beautiful messages about ourselves and ideas for unlocking our potential.

PASSIONATE PEOPLE PRODUCE Charles Kovess
Ideal for anyone considering making a living out of their passion, with some great hints for parents.

WHATEVER IT TAKES Jim Stynes, Celebrity Publishing
After costing his team a spot in the 1987 Grand Final, he went on to win the Brownlow Medal, the highest honour in Aussie Rules, and set the record for the number of consecutive games played.

MIND BODY AND SPIRIT John Douillard, Bantam Books, New York 1994
The Indian way of diet, fitness, mental approach, understanding performance and the zone – for sporting enthusiasts.

WAY OF THE PEACEFUL WARRIOR Dan Millman, HJ Kramer Inc 1984
A young man's journey trying to come to terms with life - a book about understanding manhood.

THE LIFE YOU WERE BORN TO LIVE Dan Millman
Learn more about yourself and your friends with amazing accuracy, through your birth dates.

BACK ON TRACK: DIARY OF A STREET KID Margaret Clarke, Random House, 1995
A realsitic look at life on the streets.

NEVER GIVE UP Graeme Alford, Kerr 1994
An Australian lawyer's attempts to reconstruct his life after ending up in jail following a bank robbery.

IF YOU WANT TO BE RICH AND HAPPY Don't Go To School, Robert Kiyosaki, Globe Press 1992
A critical look at our education system and well worth a read for any VCE student.

BORN TO WIN John Bertrand, Bantam 1995
The inspirational story of John Bertand's journey to winning the America's Cup on Australian II.

YOUR SACRED SELF Dr Wayne Dyer, Harper Collins 1995
A guide to your personal journey, showing how the spirit can win the battle over the ego.

SACRED HOOPS Phil Jackson, Hyperion
Chicago Bulls coach offers insights into the balance between sport and spiritualism and how it has helped him develop the most successful basketball team in American history.

THE HERO WITH A THOUSAND FACES Joseph Campbell, Princetown 1968
A book about the philosophies of Joseph Campbell.

ALL I REALLY NEEDED TO KNOW I LEARNED IN KINDERGARTEN Robert Fulghum, Grafton Books 1990
Taking human behaviour back to the simple rules you were taught in knidergarten.

THE HERO WITHIN Carol Pearson, Harper Row 1986
The mystical elements of the hero's journey with a specific female touch.

PHOTOGRAPHY CREDITS

(viii)	Lisa Saad	87	Austral
03	Wood & Mason	88	Herald Sun
04	Lisa Saad	91	Lisa Saad
06	Austral Int	92	Austral
07	Austral Int.	95	Austral
15	Lisa Saad	98	Austral
16	Serge Thomann	105	Austral
18	Austral	115	Lisa Saad
21	Jon Carnegie	116	Austral
23	Wood & Mason	119	Austral
24	Austral	122	Austral
27	Austral	130	Austral
30	Austral	132	Inside Sport
33	Herald Sun	135	Inside Sport
36	Paul West	140	Herald Sun
37	Paul West	143	Austral
39	Lisa Saad	144	Austral
40	Inside Sport	148	Austral
43	Herald Sun	157	Austral
44	Montebelli & Campbell	160	Austral
		164	Austral
51	Herald Sun	167	HeadOn
52	Austral	170	Austral
58	Austral	177	Austral
61	Austral	180	Austral
62	Austral	183	Herald Sun
66	Lisa Saad	188	Austral
72	Jon Carnegie	190	Austral
77	Inside Sport		
80	Reach		

TEXT CREDITS

01	Walt Whitman, *Leaves of Grass,* 1900
22	Time Warner
32	Bryce Courtenay, *April Fools' Day*, Mandarin 1993
35	Time Warner
41	Ian Cockerill, *Inside Sport,* July 1995
42	Delivered on the steps at the Lincoln Memorial in Washington D.C. on 28 August 1963
50	Thomas Hauser, *Muhammad Ali In Perspective,* Collins 1996
67	Theodore Roosevelt, 'It's not the critic who counts'
73	Jim Hayhurst, *The Right Mountain,* John Wiley and Sons 1997
104	Time Warner
105	Anita Roddick, *Business as Unusual,* Harper Collins
109	Kieren Perkins and Jon Carnegie, *To Be Your Best,* TGS Press 1996
110	Phil Jackson, *Sacred Hoops,* Hyperion 1995
110	Helen Keller, *The Story Of My Life,* Signet / Penguin 1988
113	Peter Howley and Steve Moneghetti, *In The Long Run,* Penguin 1996
114	Conrad Hilton, *Be My Guest,*
128	W Mitchell, *The Man Who Would Not Be Defeated,* Brolga 1995
137	Nelson Mandela, 1994 Inaugural Address
149	Michael Johnson, *Slaying The Dragon,* Hodder and Stoughton 1996
151	Kieren Perkins and Jon Carnegie, *To Be Your Best,* TGS Press 1996
156	Michael Johnson, *Slaying The Dragon,* Hodder and Stoughton 1996
161	Cathy Freeman, Sydney Press Conference, 2000
161	Peter Howley and Steve Moneghetti, *In The Long Run,* Penguin 1996
164	Phil Jackson, *Sacred Hoops,* Hyperion 1995
165	Michael Johnson, *Slaying The Dragon,* Hodder and Stoughton 1996
171	Nancy Sims, *Reach For Your Star,* Blue Mountain Arts 1996
174	Nelson Mandela, Time Warner
182	Robyn Davidson, *Tracks,* Vintage 1980
186	Dick Leider, *The Power Of Purpose*

CONTRIBUTORS

AUTHOR
JIM STYNES

Born in Ireland in 1966, Jim arrived in Australia in 1984 to try out for the Melbourne Football Club. Jim went on to win the Brownlow medal, the AFL's highest player honour, and to establish a new record for the number of consecutive games played. Jim co-founded Reach Youth in 1994 which is fast becoming one of the most influential educational institutions in the country. As a result of his work with young people, Jim has been awarded the White Flame Award and was also a member of the Youth Suicide Taskforce. Jim is married and lives in Melbourne with his wife Sam and daughter Matisse.

AUTHOR
PAUL CURRIE

Born in Melbourne in 1968, Paul completed a B.A. (Applied Science) with a major in drama in 1990. After several years training actors and directing theatrical productions, he founded the Elliott Currie Drama Studio in 1993. The studio went on to produce a host of theatrical productions and was responsible for training some of Australia's most successful performers. In 1994, Paul co-founded Reach Youth with Jim Stynes and he is still actively involved as the organisation's lead facilitator and director. Paul's most recent venture has been to direct the film One Perfect Day.

AUTHOR
JON CARNEGIE

Jon spent the early 90s writing for the Sunday Age and Sydney Morning Herald in Cambodia, Vietnam, El Salvador and Nepal. In 1995 he wrote his first book Just Passing By and started teaching at Melbourne's Trinity Grammar School. During this time, Jon also started his own business, Passionfruit Education, and was responsible for Nelson Mandela's visit to Australia in 2000. Jon's innovative teaching techniques won him a number of education prizes including the John O. Miller Award for Excellence in Education in 2000, the Commonwealth Australian Teachers Prize for Excellence and the National Excellence Award for Secondary Teaching in 2001.

PRODUCER
PHIL GREGORY

Following a successful career in marketing communications, including directorships with several leading advertising agencies, Phil moved into film and television production. In 2000 he founded Lightstream Films and is currently producing the feature movie One Perfect Day. In conjunction with business partner Jesse Martin, Phil was also responsible for producing the best-selling documentary and book, Lionheart. Phil and Jesse combined as partners and are producing the Journey of Kijana television series which is due on air in 2003. Phil has been a director of Reach since 1997. He lives in Melbourne with his wife Michelle and son, Nick.

JIM

PAUL

JON

PHIL

THANKS

Heroes has been the result of many years of work and would never have been possible without the dreams of the young people who have contributed. Thank you to all those who shared their stories with us: those who have passed through Reach and all those with whom Jon has worked in schools. We are always learning from you.

We would also like to thank publisher Sue Hines, editor Andrea McNamara and designer Katherine Chadwick at MAU Design for the production of the book.

Jon, Paul, Jim and Phil